From Bush to Bush

The Lazlo Toth Letters

Don Novello

Simon & Schuster

New York London Toronto Sydney Singapore

SIMON & SCHUSTER
Rockefeller Center
1230 Avenue of the Americas
New York, NY 10020

First Simon & Schuster trade paperback edition 2003

SIMON & SCHUSTER and colophon are registered
trademarks of Simon & Schuster, Inc.

For information about special discounts for bulk purchases,
please contact Simon & Schuster Special Sales at
1-800-456-6798 or business@simonandschuster.com

Photos on pages 23, 31, 37, 69, 74, 75, 76, 82, 114, 125,
128, 138, 154, 155 courtesy of AP/WideWorld Photos.

Designed by Red Herring Design

Manufactured in the United States of America

1 3 5 7 9 10 8 6 4 2

Library of Congress Cataloging-in-Publication Data

ISBN 0-7432-5108-3
From Bush to Bush

Dedicated to the Big Bopper.

Also by Don Novello

Lazlo Toth
P.O. Box 245
Fairfax, California
94930 U.S.A.

Vice President Elect Albert Gore
c/o U.S. Senate
Washington, D.C.

November 24, 1992

Dear Vice-President-Elect Gore,

Soon!, in less than two months, you will be going into office, and so I say, - Hello!.

I am presently working on my application for a position in the new Administration (Department of the Deficit), and am looking forward to working with you in the coming years to make the Deficit a thing of the past, once and for all! Working together, I know we can do it!

If you could two thumbs up me when my name comes up in Little Rock, I know you won't regret it! I have many ideas ready to go:

#1 - PET TAX! $200 for large Dog. $100 for medium. Small- $32. Cats- $35.

#2 — In RESTAURANTS, instead of having to just order from the menu, give people the option of being able to bring their own food and paying a "kitchen tax", for stove time, seasonings (salt and pepper),and pot and pan use. By spending less in restaurants, people will be able to save more money, and the interest on these savings will be TAXED. Also, instead of people taking food home in "doggie bags", have people write their name on the bags, and have restaurants keep the bags there (refrigerated). This way, people can come back and finish eating it at the restaurant (next day or within one week (maximum).

#3 — Instead of starting a higher (36%) tax bracket for a family that makes $200,000 or more per year, change the top rate to start at $125,000 - the annual pay of a congressman. This change will bring in a lot more revenue - there are over 400 congressmen!

#4- Let people turn in their taxes on April 17th - two days late! if they are willing to pay a $25 fine - which goes straight to pay off the deficit! This way, instead of rushing and feeling guilty for being late, they can slow down and feel patriotic. Also, this plan will help the post office by spreading out the load.

Lazlo Toth

OFFICE OF THE PRESIDENT-ELECT
AND VICE PRESIDENT-ELECT

I deeply appreciate your expression of support and encouragement. It's good to hear from you on issues of concern to you. I assure you that I will keep your views on these matters in mind.

Al

December 1, 1992

Clinton Transition Team
ATTENTION: Pres.-Elect Bill Clinton
State House
Little Rock, Arkansas

_____ TO:
  President-Elect Clinton Transition Team
_____ From:
  Lazlo Toth, California

Applying For: Employment in Clinton Administration

What Department : Department of the Deficit

What Position: Deficit Csar
  2nd choice: Deputy Deficit Csar
(If you owe somebody a favor and have to give the
top spot to him, I'll step down to the next slot.)

Starting Salary: $9 per hour (minimum).
          plus moving expenses and room and board.

_____ My Proposed Platform:
    As the Deficit Csar, or the Deputy Deficit Csar, I
vow to do all I possibly can to rid the nation of the nagging
debt that hovers over us like turkey buzzards cutting off the
sunshine so that proper light cannot even begin to reach the
budding future crops of commerce.

    Now, I'm sorry, but I have to get going. I know I
haven't got the job yet, but I'm starting to pack up and put
a few things in storage anyway. I figure once I get the word
you'll want me in D.C. - or in Little Rock, A.S.A.P. (As
Soon As Possible).

Together we can do it!

Lazlo Toth

Lazlo Toth

4 shirts
6 socks
7 underware
6 undershirt
2 ties (yellow-pink (wash)
2 shoes
1 suit (air out)
2 slippers
1 pajamas
shaving kit - toothpaste
✓ Flashlight
  ✓ DOG FOOD - BOWLS

TIME

The Presidential Inaugural Committee
requests the pleasure of your company
at
The Presidential Inaugural Parade
honoring
The President of the United States
and Mrs. Clinton
and
The Vice President of the United States
and Mrs. Gore
Wednesday, the twentieth of January
one thousand nine hundred and ninety-three
at two o'clock in the afternoon
in the City of Washington

Lazlo Toth
P.O. Box 245
Fairfax, California
94930 U.S.A.

December 10, 1992

Senator Lloyd Bentsen
c/o United States Senate
Washington, D.C.
Zip - 20510

Dear Senator Bentsen,

I saw the good news today (for you), that you were named to
be President-Elect Clinton's Treasury Secretary (if you get
confirmed, which there is no doubt in my mind), which means
I'll be working for you if I get appointed Deficit Czar or
Deputy Deficit Csar, and I just wanted to take this
opportunity to reintroduce myself in my new position,
regardless of whichever one I get.

I look forward to helping you reshape the American Economy,
and I was wondering if you have any recommendations of where
I can stay in Washington just until I rent a place of my own.

I'm not asking to stay at your house, but if you have a room
and if I wouldn't be a bother, it might be nice to spend some
private time together in your home setting.

But — Warning!, if you have male dogs, then I think it's best
that I stay with someone else. It's not that I don't like
dogs, the reason is because I have dogs of my own, and they
don't like dogs, that's our problem.

    I salute you in your new position!

    Thanks for everything,

    Lazlo Toth

    Lazlo Toth

LLOYD BENTSEN
TEXAS

United States Senate

WASHINGTON, DC 20510–4301

January 14, 1993

Dear Friend:

As you know, President-elect Clinton has asked me to become Secretary of the Treasury, and I want to take this moment to thank you for years of friendship and support.

Before a Senator can stand up and be counted, he has to have friends who will stand behind him and stand by him. You've always been there for me, and the memory of your friendship will be among the prized remembrances of my three decades in public service.

You know my decision to resign and join the Cabinet wasn't easy. Together, we've accomplished much for Texas. Together, we could do much more. But the economic challenges facing America -- challenges Texas and Texans know intimately -- are so great that I had to accept when President-elect Clinton called on me.

Through all that lies ahead, one thing will not change: my office will always be your office.

Sincerely,

Lloyd Bentsen

Lloyd Bentsen

Lazlo Toth
P. O. Box 245
Fairfax, California
94930 U.S.A.

March 25, 1993

President William Jefferson Clinton
The White House
Washington, D. C.
20500 - ZIP

Dear President Clinton,

I agree with you 100% that the Gays should not be allowed on Submarines.

P.T. boats ? - yes!

Destroyers ? - yes!

Battleships ? - yes!

Frigates ? - yes!

Submarines ? - NO!

100% American!

Lazlo Toth

Lazlo Toth

THE WHITE HOUSE
WASHINGTON

Thanks so much for writing. I welcome your thoughts and promise they will be carefully considered. I appreciate your taking the time to let me know how you feel.

Bill Clinton

U.S.

THE BILL CLINTON NOBODY KNOWS

The candidate on his values, religious faith and character
....
Can his ticket save the Democrats?

Lazlo Toth
P.O. Box 245
Fairfax, California
94930 U.S.A.

August 22, 1993

Postmaster General
U.S. Post Office Headquarters
Washington, D.C.

Dear General,

I just read that this summer (1993) is the 30th anniversary of the ZIP CODE, and it hit me like a ton of bricks that <u>NOT A THING!</u> is being done about it! Why is the U.S. postal service promoting stamps with things on them like Broadway Shows (SOUTH PACIFIC) instead of a stamp to mark an occasion that changed the American postal system forever - the invention of the ZIP CODE!

Also, I would like to know why you never write back to me? What kind of a country is this when the Postmaster General doesn't even write back! You'd think you would be the last person not to respond to somebody's letter! Isn't not answering your mail kind of like biting the hand that feeds you food? What's the problem - tired blood?

Also, why don't we have a stamp honoring THE BIG BOPPER? BUDDY HOLLY has his own stamp and so does RICHIE VALENS! BUDDY, RICHIE, and BIG performed the same last show together, and died in the same airplane crash - and two get stamps and one gets ZILCH! And now, even SOUTH PACIFIC gets one instead of him! You call this fair?

If there is a heaven, and for your sake I hope there isn't, how do you think Buddy and Richie and whoever wrote SOUTH PACIFIC feel when they run into the Big Bopper? This stamp business probably makes them very defensive. Did it ever enter your mind that your actions may have caused them embarrassment? What kind of a postal system are you running anyway?

Very disillusioned,

Lazlo Toth

Lazlo Toth

UNITED STATES POSTAL SERVICE
475 L'ENFANT PLAZA SW
WASHINGTON DC 20260-2200

September 15, 1993

Mr. Lazlo Toth
Post Office Box 245
Fairfax, CA 94930-0245

Dear Mr. Toth:

This responds to your August 22 letter about our stamp program.

Our Citizens' Stamp Advisory Committee reviews some 30,000 public suggestions each year in making final stamp selections to the Postmaster General. They focus on cultural and historical heritage, achievements, portray of natural wonders, worthy causes, issues, and interest of national concern and use the enclosed criteria in making selections. CSAC did not elect to promote the 30th anniversary of the ZIP CODE, which remains voluntary in an address.

We are proud of the variety of stamps we offer and your suggestions and ideas would be welcome by the CSAC; the enclosed sheet has their address. The CSAC could provide the reason for not selecting The Big Bopper in our rock and roll series as well.

The Postmaster General's busy schedule precludes his writing back to every one who writes. He relies upon his Vice Presidents and their staff to promptly address customer concerns for him. Our office has a fourteen day turnaround in replying to customers.

Thank your for writing.

Sincerely,

Connee L. Rainey
Senior Consumer Affairs Associate

Enclosures

Reference:32510557:seb

Catholics for Jesus

Box 245 Fairfax, California 94930 USA

LAZLO TOTH
Decorating Committee
ReconStruction

January 22, 1994

Pope John Paul II Wojtyla
The Vatican
Vatican City (State)

Dear Your Holiness,

My best regards for the New Year - 1994!
Who would ever think that the time would come when the
futuristic year 1 9 8 4 would be ten years ago! It baggles
my mind!
If life is just a matter of TIME, and TIME is just
man's way of measuring DECAY, it seems to me that things are
moving along right on schedule.

But!, Holiness!, I've been troubled lately thinking
about something, and I thought I'd go to the top (You!) for
the answer. My parish Priest (Father Mick) is of NO HELP
WHATSOEVER, believe me. I heard he got upset recently when a
restaurant in San Franciso wouldn't give him a FREE MEAL.
Everyone knows Italain restaurants always let Priests and
Policemen eat for free, "BUT NOT WHEN YOU'RE ON A DATE!",
they told him.

I heard the news today that the Hubble telescope, which
I knew would lead to no good, reported back information that
translated to the fact that there are 20 billion planets that
could support life in our universe. Twice as many planets
that scientist thought before Hubble. And even if there is
life on only one tenth of one percent of those planets, it
still adds up to hundreds of thousands of planets with life
on them. HUNDREDS of THOUSANDS!

Holiness!, my question: If there are other people on
other planets, when they die, do they go to the same heaven
we go to, or does each planet have it's own heaven?

I sure hope Earth has its own Heaven, so we don't have
to be with a bunch of PIN HEADS who, besides maybe not even
remotely looking like us, may not even speak one of our many
languages.
Your Holiness, with a "Big Enough for the Whole Universe
Size Heaven", you could spend three lifetimes there, and
chances are, you probably would not run into even ONE PERSON
you knew back on EARTH.

As a Catholic, I feel that it's pretty dissapointing,
thinking we try to live a good life so we can get to Heaven,
and then find out we have to share it with everybody and his
brother. Why would God do this to us?

Laylo Toth

Lazlo Toth
P.O. Box 245
Fairfax, California
94930 U.S.A.

March 20, 1995

LaMar Alexander
Presidential Candidate and Former Governor of Tennessee
Knoxville, Tennessee.

Dear Candidate LaMar (TheOcean) Alexander,

Welcome to the 1996 Presidential race! Come aboard!
So far there is yourself, SENATOR PHIL GRAMS of Texas,
PAT BUCHANON- the right wing moderator, ROBERT DOLE, Jerry
Ford's Bicentennial running mate, Congressman ROBERT "Bombs
Away!" DORNAN, and I just heard on the radio that Governor
PETE WILSON, who promised us, <u>four months ago</u>, when he was
running for Governor, that he would serve his full four years
if he was elected Governor, is now "thinking" about running.
Lamar, is it any wonder why people equate politicians
with Zoo Dung?

I would like to see Wilson have to go up against O. J.
Simpson's lawyer, F. Lee Bailey - it would be <u>Marine to
Marine</u>.
<u>Bailey:</u> Governor, what else have you forgotten in
the last four months? Can you remember any other promises
you may have forgotten?
If you get elected President, do you promise not to quit, and
announce after four months that you're "thinking" about
running for POPE? You would be the first Marine Pope. You
could wear Camouflage robes! You could be the first Pope to
visit a country by landing on the beach!

<u>Judge Ito</u>: That's enough, Mr. Bailey. I want you BOTH
to sit down. Oh?, you're already sitting down? I mean,
stand up!, let everybody see how short some Marines are.
I'm mean, no, you're not THAT short, - yes, compared to
Marcia Clarke you're both short, but compared to that waste
basket over there, you're both TALL. Not REAL tall, but
taller than some of O.J.'s golf clubs. That's a good one,
did you get that one, Marcia? It was just like Deja Vous all
over again, oh, did I say that before?

TheOcean! Sir! Changing back the subject. You have
many rivers to cross, LeMar, and here is some sound advice:
- <u>Loose the plaid shirt</u>, Hunters are not going
  to vote for you.
- <u>Loose the "Come On along" tag</u>. Dole has a lock on the
  ragtime music fans.
- <u>Stop</u> using <u>two</u> different <u>names</u>. Some of you campaign
  material say's LAMAR, some say's <u>Alexander</u> — CHOOSE ONE!

Your advertising campaign is confusing so far. It's a bad
start for a good man. ReGroup!
You can win if you get enough votes, that's the key!

Lazlo Toth

 *Come on along!*
Alexander
PRESIDENT

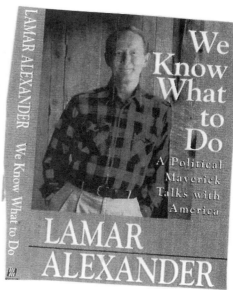

May 23, 1995

Mr. Lazlo Toth
P.O. Box 245
Fairfax, California 94930

Dear Mr. Toth,

I was delighted to receive your letter and please excuse my late response. I have included my correct address since I am currently living and working in Nashville, Tennessee.

Your kind words were quite encouraging, and I deeply appreciate your generous donation—you have brought us even closer to our year-end goal of $20 million.

It was kind of you to share your insight as to what it takes to win a presidential election. Your final words may prove prophetic indeed!

Please keep in touch—you can reach me at the campaign address listed below.

Very best wishes.

Sincerely,

Lamar

Lamar Alexander

LA/rg

P.S.   I have enclosed a campaign button, as well as a sticker which you can place on the rear bumper of your car.

Campaign Headquarters
1808 West End Avenue, Suite 600
Nashville, Tennessee 37203
615/327-3350
Fax 615/340-0397

Paid for by Alexander for President, Inc.
Contributions are not deductible for federal income tax purposes.

Finance Office
1808 West End Avenue, Suite 928
Nashville, Tennessee 37203
615/327-3270
Fax 615/327-1480

Lazlo Toth
P.O. Box 245
Fairfax, California
94930 U.S.A.

April 9, 1995

Governor Pete Wilson
Part Time Governor of California
Sacramento, California

Dear Governor Wilson,

I would have written you sooner but what's the difference since you've been out of the state so much, you probably wouldn't have gotten it anyway.

The original reason I've been meaning to write is to tell you about an idea I have that can solve two of California's biggest problems: <u>Illegal Immigration</u>, and the <u>crowding of state prisons</u>.

Here's the idea - it's kind of self explanatory - it's called: <u>THREE STRIKES AND YOU'RE A BORDER GUARD</u>.

I give you this idea FREE, because I love my state and would not stab it in the back like YOU! did, by going back on your promise that you wouldn't run for President if you were re-elected Governor, And, Now!,you don't even have the decency to Quit! being Governor, but want us to continue paying you as Governor as you galavant around the country running for President which you have about a ZERO! percent chance of winning! Not after THE BIG LIE! And not after the rest of nation finds out that besides lacking honor, you also lack a personality. That's a bad combo.

All you had to do to be President was to sit back and do a good job as Governor, then Dole could have "drafted" you to be his V.P., and then, win or loose, you would still be a contender to be President someday.

But now, because you went back on your promise, BECAUSE YOU LIED!, you won't even win the California primary! Your own state!
After '96, you won't be just a lame duck, you'll be a Cooked Goose! If there's another baseball strike, you won't even be able to get a job as a REPLACEMENT FAN!

May the lord have mercy on you and your advisors. It looks to me now like Huffington is California's only hope.

Lazlo Toth

Lazlo Toth

GOVERNOR'S OFFICE

April 18, 1995

Mr. Lazlo Toth
P.O. Box 245
Fairfax, California 94930

Dear Mr. Toth:

Many thanks for your letter sharing your thoughts regarding my possible candidacy for the Presidency of the United States. I appreciate your taking the time to express your views on this important subject.

Please know that I have simply formed an exploratory committee to seek and accept support for my candidacy for President of the United States. I expect to make my final decision as to whether I will formally enter the race in the near future.

As you know, the past five years have presented many challenges. Nonetheless, California has provided a model for the federal government in government reform and deficit reduction. In fact, according to members of the Governor's Council of Economic Advisors at Stanford's Hoover Institute, headed by George M. Shultz, if the federal government had been imposing the same kind of spending cuts and the same sort of fiscal discipline that California has, the federal government would now be running a surplus rather than growing a deficit.

And please know that I'm fully committed to doing my job as Governor of California and know that my first duty is to the citizens of California. We have a very aggressive program that I proposed in my State of the State -- a program we plan on completing.

My goal is to continue to fight to make government work more efficiently and effectively for our state's citizens. However, somewhere along the way, our leaders and our government have lost track of the bedrock values that built this great country. We should reward hard work, not idleness...promote individual opportunity, not group remedies...and demand that people are held

Governor Pete Wilson

GOVERNOR PETE WILSON • SACRAMENTO, CALIFORNIA 95814

accountable for their actions. It's wrong to reward illegal immigrants for violating our borders and breaking our laws or to indulge in reverse discrimination by conferring special privileges based on race and gender. It's wrong to release hardened career criminals onto our streets to hurt other victims, and for our welfare system to warehouse dependency instead of rewarding individual initiative.

It's an outrage to use your hard-earned tax dollars to support all this nonsense. As you well know, this is no way to reward people who work hard, pay their taxes, and obey the laws of this country.

Obviously, there are no quick-fix solutions to the many challenges facing our great state and nation. Please know that I will continue to do what's right for all Californians and the United States. That's what we're doing, and be assured that's what we'll continue to do.

Again, thank you for your letter.

Sincerely,

PETE WILSON

The Emu Foundation

Securing the future of the second largest nonflying bird in nature.

Office of the Vice President

P.O. Box 245 / Fairfax, Calfiornia / 94978 / USA

July 27, 1995

United States Ambassador
American Embassy
Ankara, Turkey

Dear Mr. Ambassador,

Thank you for reading this letter. I will get right to the point.

Last night at our weekly meeting, I came up with the idea of raffling off tickets for "TURKEY IN TURKEY". It would be Thanksgiving (Turkey) dinner in Turkey, (the country).

The prize would include round trip airplane tickets to Turkey, plus clean Hotel for two days, and on Thanksgiving Day, a full course Thanksgiving dinner, with roast turkey, mashed potatoes, cranberry sauce, and beverage.

Mr. Ambassador, could you please tell me where I might make arrangements for this dinner? Do you think any major medium priced clean hotel in Ankara or Istanbul would offer a turkey dinner on Thanksgiving Day, or do I have to make special arrangments with one of your staff? I would like to avoid going through Washington if it's at all possible. It's just simpler to handle it this way. I guess it would be possible for us to pack up the meal and send it with them (the winners), but then we have to consider the possibility of some kind of meat inspection at customs, and I don't know if a cooked meal like that could pass mustard on a flight that long.

Thank you for all your help. I know that by working together, side by side, we can do it! If I can be of any help to you on this side of the pond, please feel free to call upon me.

Lazlo Toth

Lazlo Toth

Embassy of the United States of America

American Embassy Ankara
PSC 93 Box 5000
APO AE 09823

September 12, 1995

Mr. Lazlo Toth
Vice President, The Emu Foundation
P.O. Box 245
Fairfax, CA 94978

Dear Mr. Toth:

Ambassador Grossman asked me to reply to your letter concerning your fundraising effort, "Turkey in Turkey."

Most of the American hotel chains in Istanbul or Ankara, such as the Hilton, the Sheraton, or the Ramada Renaissance, offer a traditional Turkey dinner on Thanksgiving. A hotel reservation agent in the United States could give you details and prices.

As an alternative, I might suggest that you have your winners join the Friends of ARIT Thanksgiving trip to Antalya. ARIT stands for the American Research Institute in Turkey and they are engaged in archeological research here. The Friends of ARIT is an international group interested in archeology that plan trips to various sites. The Thanksgiving trip to Antalya on the Mediterranean Sea is an ARIT tradition and the Sheraton Hotel there gives us a very good rate as well as preparing an outstanding Thanksgiving meal. For approximately $400 each, your winners could join in an American Thanksgiving and then travel with the group to see famous sights in the area. Although this year's trip is not final, the group will be traveling to Myra to visit the Church of St. Nicholas, the Bishop who is the source of the Santa Claus legend. I am enclosing a flyer from last year's trip for your information. If you are interested in this alternative, you can contact Dr. Toni Cross, ARIT-Ankara Director, c/o the American Embassy in Ankara.

You should also know that Turkish Airlines (THY) charges the same fare ($722) from New York to any place in Turkey so the fare from New York to Istanbul is the same as the fare from New York to Antalya.

I would like to add a cautionary note. It is a long flight to Turkey and people generally suffer from jet lag for a few days after they arrive. If your winners were to arrive on

Wednesday, November 22nd, they would probably not feel much like eating a big turkey dinner the next day. Further it would be such a shame for them to make such a long flight and not have a chance to see any of the wonders of this country.

I hope this information is of assistance to you in making your plans. If I can answer any further questions, please contact me again.

Sincerely,

Michael Ann Dean

Ms. Michael Ann Dean
Community Liaison Office Coordinator

cc: The Ambassador
ADM - Bill Eaton

Lazlo Toth
P. O. Box 245
Fairfax, California
94930 U.S.A.

December 7, 1996

President Bill Clinton
The White House
Washington, D.C.

Dear President Clinton,

You are making a BIG mistake sending American ground troops into Bosnia-Hertzagovinia. Those people have been fighting among each other for almost 900 years and sending American soldiers there, even if they're called "peace keepers", will not bring peace to the region.

In ancient times it was the Hertzo's against the Govinias, then they joined together and turned on the Bosnians, and at times the Croats, the Serbians and even the Montenegrans and the Albanians have been dragged back and forth into the mess.

But! the problem is not politics, it is RELIGION!

Some are Muslim, some are Orthodox Catholics, others have Greek-Catholic blood, and still others come from various pentecoastal-intramountainous backgrounds too numerous to mention and even harder to spell.

Mr. President, the only way to solve this problem once and for all is with a plan for a new multi-religion inspired religion.

We must go in with a RELIGIOUS OBJECTIVE, not a military one! We must unite the whole region into one united combinations of religions, so that they will be willing to worship together, on the same day of the week, and STOP FIGHTING!

To this I suggest - WEDNESDAY.

No current religion observes WEDNESDAY as the sabbath! Friday, yes! (Moslem) - Saturday, yes! (Jewish), Sunday, yes!, (Christian). But Wednesday is not taken. This is the cornerstone of my plan!

I would be willing to have a go at coming up with some kind of a Moslem-Christian-semi-Orthodox geographically inspired "Bill-of-Rights-of-Beliefs", and going in there with a blueprint for a meshing, if you give me the nod to go ahead. I will do it for "Expenses Only" (no salary), on a "Bonus-if-Pleased Basis". I will travel incognitio, wearing my own dry cleaner tag free (untraceable) clothing. All that I need from you is a United Nations passport, one of those powder blue berets, and a beeper.

I want the right to have somebody there if I have to be vaccinated,

THE WHITE HOUSE

WASHINGTON

January 31, 1996

Mr. Lazlo Toth
Post Office Box 245
Fairfax, California 94930

Dear Lazlo:

I appreciate hearing your views regarding the situation in the former Yugoslavia.

With the help of decisive American leadership, the warring parties in Bosnia have reached an agreement to end their conflict. On November 21, in Dayton, Ohio, they made a commitment to peace, agreeing to put down their guns, to preserve Bosnia as a single state, to investigate and prosecute war criminals, to protect the human rights of all citizens, and to try to build a peaceful, democratic future. Now, continued American participation is essential to end the death and suffering there and to prevent the war from resuming and spreading throughout the region.

America's role in Bosnia is not to fight a war, but to help the Bosnian people secure their own peace agreement. Stability in Central Europe is important to our security, and in the post-Cold War era, it remains critical for the United States to continue asserting leadership effectively.

More than twenty-five other nations, including our major NATO allies, have pledged to take part. They will contribute about two-thirds of the total implementation force. The mission is precisely defined with clear, realistic goals that can be achieved in about a year. American troops will take their orders only from the American general who commands NATO. They will have the authority to respond immediately, as well as the training and the equipment to respond with overwhelming force to any threat to their own safety or any violations of the military provisions of the peace agreement. With our leadership and the commitment of our allies, the people of Bosnia can have the chance to decide their future in peace.

Thank you for your interest in this critical issue.

Sincerely,

Bill Clinton

Things That Go Clique-Claque in the Night

The death of Dean Martin brings one step closer the end of that sine qua non of Camelot hip, the Rat Pack, one of the three great 20th century circles of friends

Lazlo Toth
P. O. Box 245
Fairfax, California
94930 U.S.A.

January 5,

RAT PACK

Members Included:
- Singer Frank Sinatra
- Singer Dean Martin
- Singer Sammy Davis Jr.
- Comedian Joey Bishop
- Actress Shirley MacLaine
- Actor Tony Curtis
- President John Kennedy

Editor and Chief
TIME MAGAZINE
Time and Life Building
Rockefeller Center
New York, NY 10020

Dear Editor and Chief,

People rely on TIME magazine for accurate reporting, and in the past, I've included myself among this misled group. What changed my mind, and made my views take a U-ee, was an article in this weeks, Neut Gringrich, Time's man of the end of the Year issue.

The article was about the RAT PACK, and it listed "Tony Curtis" among its "members".

How does something like this happen? Tony Curtis in the Rat Pack? I couldn't believe my eyes.

And besides the Tony Curtis blunder, you left out one of the top legitimate founding members, Peter Lawford!

I guess we should be happy you didn't leave out Joey Bishop and Sammy Davis Jr. and list Sigfried and Roy instead.

In the future, when someone goes to the library, doing research on that time in history, when they look up "RAT PACK", they will find your article which incorrectly lists "Tony Curtis" among the "Member's Included".

And this misinformation will be passed along, it will be reprinted, and it will multiply. And eventually, electronically!, it will travel past our planet's pull, and move through space, in Truth's place, unjustly imbedded in the living library of the circle of time.

And someone, someone there!, is responsible. Should they make amends in some manner? Yes! But basically, unfortunately, the harm is done. As far as the factual data on the Rat Pack is concerned, the harm is done.

Over and Out,

Lazlo Toth

TIME

Patrick Smith
Editorial Offices

Time Inc.

Time
Time & Life Building
Rockefeller Center
New York, NY 10020-1393

212-522-1212

February 2, 1996

Dear Mr. Toth:

Thank you for your letter in response to the January 8 Chronicles item on the Rat Pack. Though Tony Curtis' (admittedly very tenuous) connection with the Sinatra clan remains a matter of contention among woolly headed gossip columnists, the omission of hard-core Packer Peter Lawford from the membership roll was an oversight. We regret the lapse, and we appreciated your bringing it to our attention.

Our thanks, again, for writing. Ring-a-ding-ding.

Sincerely,

Patrick Smith

Mr. Lazlo Toth
PO Box 245
Fairfax, CA   94930
PS:sf

January 21, 1996

Police Chief Fred Lau
San Francisco Police Department
850 Bryant Headquarters
San Francisco, California

Dear Chief,

Congradulations on being named Police Chief by Mayor Brown.

I read that you wanted to be a policeman so bad that you hung up side down by your feet for two days to try to stretch yourself two inches so that you could reach the height requirement necessary to qualify for the SF police department. With determination like that, I knew you weren't the type to resign just because of all the hooplala that's come up in the last few days about your resume.

Mayor Brown tried to defend you by saying, "everybody lies on their resume". But it turns out you didn't "lie".
You said you were an "alumnus" of San Francisco State, you didn't say you graduated! And, like the newspapers are now saying, according to the dictionary, the term "Alumnus" means, "a person who has <u>attended</u> or graduated from a school", and that clearly includes people that are six to nine units shy of a degree, like yourself.

I consider myself practically an alumnus of SFS myself since I used to drive past there all the time when I was taking a Karaoke class from a woman who lived out near the airport. It's a fine school, and they keep the grounds looking very nice.
And I'll bet the neighborhood will become a lot safer next semester when you go back to pick up those nine units you're lacking. There's nothing better to deter crime than having a student who also is the POLICE CHIEF walking around campus. Especially if you have a dog with you.
I just hope you won't go signing up for a lot of extracurricular activities - after class, we need you behind your desk at Headquarters, not hanging out at the student union!

<u>One suggestion</u> - don't buy one of those book bag back packs. People do not want to see a Police Chief wearing one of those,

Laslo Toth

Lazlo Toth

FRED H. LAU
CHIEF OF POLICE

January 26, 1996

Lazlo Toth
P.O. Box 245
Fairfax, CA 94930

Dear Mr. Toth:

I want to thank you for your kind expression of congratulations on my appointment to Chief of Police. It is an honor and privilege to serve the citizens of San Francisco and I am sincerely grateful for your confidence and support.

There cannot be change without commitment and we have a commitment to change. There are many tasks to accomplish and I pledge to you that we will reach our goals.

Once again, thank you and best wishes for the New Year!

Sincerely,

FRED H. LAU
Chief of Police

LAZLO TOTH
P.O. BOX 245
FAIRFAX, CA.

February 1, 1996

Mr. Steve Forbes
P.O. Box 1009
Bedminister NJ 07921

Dear Steve Forbes,

I've seen your magazine at the Library, and now I get to meet the real man. Glad to know you. You sure have kicked up some dust in the last few weeks.

You came riding into the Iowa primary on a horse called Flat Tax, and the posse chasing Dole you were part of, turned out chasin' you.

Now, even Dole, the front runner, is running scared. They say he's thinking he might have to go back to Philip Morris or the Oscar Meyer people to beg for more money to pay for more advertising.

And he's afraid he's going to be locked up in Washington, stuck gardening the Budget mess, while you're out grass rooting in Iowa, smoozing in the suburbs, and trotting around to all the radio and Tv stations, buying up all the air time.

Yes, Dole is scared. Yes, he is threatened! Your money is working, your message is taking root! Stand tall! Bravo!

Forbes!, If you come in second in the Iowa primary, you're going to be a real contender, and you've got to have more of a platform than just FLAT TAX. Nobody takes a candidate who talks about the same topic all the time, very seriously for very long.

So, here is a great idea for another topic for you:
<u>VOICE MAIL STINKS</u>

Like most of so called "modern technology", it mainly benefits Business, not people.

They <u>tricked</u> us into thinking we were getting something "More Advanced", but we just got something less human.

They took away the people and put BRICK WALLS at the other end of the line.

Forbes, I like to listen to <u>Music</u>, but on the <u>RADIO</u>, not the <u>telephone</u>!

Forbes!, Using the telephone in these "more advanced" times,is like standing in a bread line.
<u>We've become a Nation of people waiting for the BEEP.</u>

Forbes!, If you want to <u>Make Dole Mulch</u> , put the FLAT TAX on the back burner, and come out as the candidate who thinks <u>VOICE MAIL STINKS</u>!

I am loaning you $1 CASH to help finance your campaign.

<u>Everyone</u> HATES Voice Mail, You Can Win.

TOTH!

FOR PRESIDENT

March 7, 1996

Mr. Lazlo Toth
PO Box 245
Fairfax, CA 94930

Dear Mr. Toth,

Thank you so very much for your generous contribution to my campaign. I deeply appreciate your support.

We will not let up now. We will continue our efforts to reach more and more Americans with our message of growth and optimism.

My reason for seeking the presidency is to unlock the stranglehold that the political class has on American life. I am an outsider who knows firsthand the promise of a new economy, who sees how government is dragging down all Americans and is determined to change it.

I believe you and I share the same vision of an unshackled future, a future that embraces all the wonderful opportunities of a new economy.

Thank you again for your support and your belief in the winning ideas of this campaign. Together, we can move America forward to an era of unparalleled prosperity.

Cordially,

Steve Forbes

PO Box 1009 • 1400 Rt. 206 North • Bedminster, New Jersey 07921 • 908-781-5111 • 1-800-820-6300
E-Mail: forbes@forbes96.com • www.forbes96.com

Paid for by Forbes for President Committee, Inc.. Contributions are not deductible as charitable for federal tax purposes.

February 14, 1996

Senator Phil Gramm
Gramm for President Headquarters
P.O. Box 33119
Washington, D.C.

LAZLO TOTH
P.O. BOX 245
FAIRFAX, CA

Dear Former Candidate Gramm,

Any man that lists his hidden talent as "target shoting" is okay in my booklet. But the voters have spoken!, and face it!, people just don't seem to like you.

But, STILL, I don't like what you did to the NRA! They gave you a ton of money, and after just two semi-humiliating defeats, in two semi-obscure states, you throw in the towel!

This is going to be one Valentine's Day the NRA will want to forget.

I just hope you can get re-elected to the Senate so you can make it up to them. But now, I don't know. Not after how you got steamrolled by Pat Buchanon, the second rate journalist, who's sole qualification for the Presidency is that he used to caddy and make Highballs for President Nixon.

Once they put him in charge of a party they gave for Nixon during his last day's. They say Nixon was a wreck, and they just wanted him to relax, to have a few drinks and hear a few jokes.

Buchanon tries to start the ball rolling and asks Nixon, "Mr. President, why did the chicken cross the road?".

They say Nixon turned WHITE, his hands started shaking, and then he said, "It was raining . . my wipers weren't working properly . . . I wasn't even driving . . . I didn't know it was a chicken . . I thought it was a cat . . it felt like a cat.", and then he hollared "JUST..LEAVE... ME ALONE!", and guzzled down his drink and left the room.

They say that's the last time they gave Buchanon any responsibilty.

But, enough about him, let's get back to YOU! Congressman Dornan got a total of 111 votes in IOWA, less votes than the average Hight School Homecoming Queen receives, but he didn't QUIT! He's going on to New Hamshire like a MAN, - He's no QUITTER.

Anyway, good luck in your re-election campaign for the Senate.

Here's a dollar for a button, now it's a collectors item. Senator, you must have a lot leftover, so, if it's not asking too much, could you send two?

Lazlo Toth

WEDNESDAY, FEBRUARY 14, 1996

Gramm Calling It Quits
GOP's Iowa survivors move on to New Hampshire

Steve
Forbes
Wants a
Flat Tax.
Do You?

EMERGENCY REPLY

Dear Steve,

I understand the importance of the upcoming primaries. This is a critical period for us and I want to help.
That's why I am enclosing my special contribution of: another topic for your campaign
NOBODY TAKES CHRONIC FATIGUE SYNDROM SERIOUSLY. Please make check payable to

❏ $10 ❏ $15 ❏ $20 ❏ $_____ Other Forbes for President
Combined with the FLAT TAX, and ANTI-VOICE MAIL ideas, your
message is now a philosophy ready to go! Onward to San Diego!

FIRST CLASS MAIL PERMIT NO. 26 BEDMINSTER, NJ
POSTAGE WILL BE PAID BY ADDRESSEE

Laszlo Toth

Toth
45
A 94978-0245

STEVE FORBES FOR PRESIDENT
PO BOX 1018
BEDMINSTER NJ 07921-9954

Mr. Lazlo Toth
P.O. Box 245
Fairfax, CA 94978-0245

★★★ DOLE
FOR PRESIDENT

February 28,

Senator Bob Dole for President
810 First Street N.E.
Washington, D.C. 20002

Dear Bob,

Yes! you came in second yesterday in Arizona behind
Steve Forbes, but! you won in both the Dakotas. In my
opinion, finally!,the "real" Bob Dole is back on the boat!

So far the former Watergate bat boy Pat Buchanan has
won in Louisiana, Iowa and New Hampshire, but now, at last!,
you too have won a primary. Bob, I don't have to tell you,
it was looking <u>bleek</u>.

I think the main reason you're getting such a slow
start is because of the comments you made in Iowa regarding
your "favorite song". I saw the speech on C-Span.

You told the crowd,
"Did you hear that song they played when I came into the
hall?".
'It's called, "<u>I'll Never Walk Alone</u>". It's my favorite
song".
You said, "When I was recovering from my war wound,
sometimes I would listen to that song 30 or forty times a
day."

Senator!, the name of the song is "<u>You'll</u> Never Walk
Alone", not, <u>I'll </u>never walk alone! How could you listen to
it 30 or 40 times a day and not even know the correct title?
It made people start thinking that you were not telling
the truth about that being your favorite song and that you
just said it was becuase that's the song the band played when
you walked in, like jokesters use to tell the band to play
<u>Mac the Knife </u>for President Nixon.

Anyway, even if you got the words right, I don't think
people want a President who's favorite song is "<u>You'll Never
Walk Alone</u>". It's just too down and slow and depressing.

I am now in the process of searching for a new favorite
song for you, and I can assure you, it will be a <u>positive,</u>
very UP!, happy tune.

At present, I'm experimenting adapting your message to
the tune, "Goin' to a Go-Go", but it remains to be seen if
the original writers will approve the new lyrics.

Lazlo Toth

Junior Wednesday, March 6, 1996

Governor George Bush Jr. III
Governor of Texas
Austin, Texas

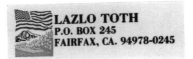
LAZLO TOTH
P.O. BOX 245
FAIRFAX, CA. 94978-0245

Dear Governor Bush Jr.,

I write to thank you for endorsing Robert Dole and
helping him win 7 out of 7 primaries yesterday on Junior
Tuesday. You may think that your endorsement wouldn't be
appreciated by people outside the high cotton, low tar crowd,
but let me just say, on my own recognizance, thank you! from
nearby the bottom of my heart.

If you were standing in front of me now, instead of
rivers and states away, I would say, "Governor, Let me take
you out to dinner, and let me fill your plate as we stroll
down the line of Ponderosa cuisine, and don't you dare put
your hand anywhere near your wallet — the meal's on me,
benerage included".

You helped us win our junior victory by getting behind
our front runner, which helped clear the field, so that
Senator Dole can now concentrate on beating Clinton and not
have to respond to cheap commercials from desperate third
rate PITCHFORK! Candidates (Buchanon), who call themselves
REPUBLICANS, and should QUIT! and go home and work on their
scrapbook, instead of staying in the race and forcing our
aging choice to keep going around the country always having
to talk about his arm, and having people expect him to know
the words to every popular song since the turn of the century
started.

Come on! He knew the name of the song was "You'll Never
Walk Alone, not I'll, he knew that, he was tired!
If you had to be in New Hampshire and Iowa on the same
day, you would be tired, too.
And someday you will know first hand how hard it is.

This is my prediction: You will be the first President's
son to become President yourself since John Q. Adams!
Yes!, the second President Bush will be YOU!, President
George Bush Junior the Third!
There's only one other young republican candidate on the
political horizon who I think you have you watch out for, and
I think you know who I mean - your brother, Jebs!
He's a Bush, too, and he wants to be President, too, you
know that. Personally, I see nothing wrong with both of you
mounting the mantle, Bush after Bush, but I just hope Jebs
understands you get to be President first! Break the natural
order, and you end up in a Fredo Corleone situation, and
nobody needs that, he's smart, too.
Besides, you're going to need him in Florida, and to
oversee things in Cuba, once things start up again.

Governor!, On behalf of supporters of Senator Bob Dole,
thanks a million for the boost! Lazlo Toth

Governor Bush
COMMITTEE ★

April 4, 1996

Lazlo Toth
Post Office Box 245
Fairfax, California 94978

Dear Lazlo Toth,

Thank you for your letter supporting my endorsement of Senator Bob Dole for the Republican Presidential nomination.

To continue our efforts to change America, we must change Presidents. I am convinced Senator Dole is the best choice for Texas. He understands Texans can run Texas, and will work to return power and authority to our state and communities.

Bob Dole can win and move our country in the right direction. His conservative philosophy, character, and views on the issues mark him as a leader in tune with Texas and ready to lead America.

Thank you for your letter and for your support of a good man, Bob Dole.

Sincerely,

George W. Bush

Political Advertisement paid for by Governor Bush Committee, 807 Brazos, Suite 800, Austin, Texas 78701. Phone (512)472-2874, Fax (512)322-9896. Allan Shivers, Jr., Treasurer.

Lazlo Toth
Post Office Box 245
Fairfax, California 94978

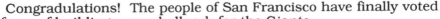

Mr. Peter Magowan
President, San Francisco Giants
c/o Candlestick (3-Com) Park
San Francisco, California 94124

Dear Mr. Magowan,

  Congradulations! The people of San Francisco have finally voted in favor of building a new ballpark for the Giants.
  Four times before the measure went down in defeat, but like a sea lion that seldom comes up for air, victory finally showed its hairy head. And now, if all goes well, if you're able to raise the $225 million you say you can, come the spring of the year 2000, your dream will slide into reality, and you will cut the red ribbon, and shout, "Play Ball!".
  What a way to start a new millinium!

  The papers say you hope to get some of the $225 million by selling the stadium's name (Clorox Field?), and by selling Beer and Wine "pour" rights, and food "chew" rights.
  Regarding the issue of home runs being hit over the right field fence into the Bay, your right hand man, Larry Baer, said, "major league baseballs float in water", and he said that you might hire someone who would go into the Bay in an inner tube and retrieve the balls with a net.
  Mr. Magowan, you thought you would have to "hire" someone to do this job, and instead, I will pay you.
  YES!, I would like to BUY! the <u>Rights to Retrieve Baseballs Hit Over the Right Field Wall into the Bay.</u>

  No!, I am not planning to plunge into the Bay with a net in some stupid inner tube. Instead, I will manage a Baseball Retrieving Canine Swimming Team from a "Dog Dugout", located on land, or floating in shallow waters, right outside the right field wall.
  My dogs and I will watch the game on a large television screen from our dugout, and the moment I see a ball sail over the right field wall, I will press my remote control dugout door opener, and my mixed breed team will be off! - jumping into the bay, swimming towards the floating homer. The first dog to reach the ball will snag it (by mouth), and with his team mates barking by his side, dog paddle the wet homer to shore.

  MY OFFER: I will sell advertising space on the canine wet suits that my Baseball Retrieving Swimming Team will wear. It may be the name of a dog food company (like Gravy Train), or an airline (like Lufthansa). And I will make an independant televison (or Internet) deal to permit my team to be seen in action retrieving the floating homers.
  For this <u>Aquatic Home Run Retrieval Francise</u> I offer to pay the Giants organization $1000 per year plus one third of my revenues, minus the cost of water bowls, fresh towels, snacks, and other expenses.

    I wait for your reply,

    Lazlo Toth

PETER A. MAGOWAN
PRESIDENT AND
MANAGING GENERAL PARTNER

April 19, 1996

Mr. Lazlo Toth
P. O. Box 245
Fairfax, CA 94978

Dear Lazlo:

    I loved your offer to provide a canine retrieval service for home runs hit into the water at our new ballpark. Your dogs will become the best known canines in the country! The Giants stand ready to discuss (on land) your proposal at any time that is convenient for you. And thanks again for your brilliant suggestion!

        Sincerely,

Peter A. Magowan

PAM/sbc

cc: Larry Baer
      Pat Gallagher

TOTHWORKS
FILM STUDIO/ARBORETUM

April 19, 96

Daniel Rosty Rostenkowski
Former Chairman House Ways and Means Committee
Chicago, Ilinois

Dear Rosty,

It's just not fair! What did you do that the rest
didn't? Yes, they dropped the 17 counts of corruption, and
charged you instead with just 2 counts of "mail fraud", and
even though you'll get to go to one of those "Club Fed"
slipper slammers, with the lighted Bocce ball courts, and
cable T.V., what did you do to become their slav sacrifice?
Isn't the first lady from Illinois? She couldn't help you
out? Please!
But, Rosty, on the bright side: When you're
incarcerated, you'll have time to write your book! And, if
you're willing to write a "Tell-all", no holes barred,
"confession" type book, you could get five million for it,
easy. And when you tell them my studio is already interested
in buying the film rights, we could share a half a million
more.

This is how it shoud start:
The cathredral is dark, only candles.
Rosty Rostenkowski enters. He dips his ball park frank
size fingers in the murky holy water, and does a quick knee
dip kind of genuflection light before he enters the dark
confessional. He kneels, waiting for the screen to slide
back. He smells the Priest's cabbage roll breathe, before
he sees the sharp, weasel shaped face of Father Stan Dwitzel.
"This is going to be easy", you say to yourself. You know
Dwitzel is going to recognize your voice and he'll give you a
light penance, probably two Hail Mary's and one Our Father
for each count of corruption.
Rosty pulls out his calculator, but before he can punch in
17 times two,, Dwitzel starts coughing, he wants to begin.

Rostenkowski (Duval) remembers years before when the
Priest's uncle, Joe Dwitzel, called him, asking if he could
help get his young seminarian nephew a summer job at the
Tribune. But Rosty got him a job with the City instead.
Burning leaves. That summer, Stanley was the highest paid
seminarian in Cook County.
But now it's time to begin - Dwitzel is ready.
Softly, you (Duval) begin your confession:
"Forgive me Father, for I have sinned. I have served 36
years in the Congress of the United States."

The money people will want Danny Aiello or Tom Arnold to
play you, but Duval is my first choice, even though the
budget goes way up. We'll probably settle for Nick Nolte, we
can live with Nolte. And when you (Nolte) gets on the plane
to fly off to prison, and we hear Elton Johns singing the
title song, Daniel my Brother, IT'S OSCAR TIME!

Call me as soon as possible, I'm ready to run with this.

Laszlo Toth

Pat Buchanon
6862 Elm St. Suite 210
McLean Va. 22101

April 22. 1996

Mr. Lazlo Toth
PO Box 245
Fairfax CA 94978-0245

Dear Pat,

A possum was found dead! with suspecious "mountain lion like teeth marks" on his abdomen, and what happens? Two days later, voters defeat! the measure that would have permitted hunters to legally kill mountain lions once again in California.

What do voters think is going to happen after the lions eat all the possums and racoons? Do they have to wait until one of these pythons with paws come down from the hills and pounces on people at Starbucks?

Okay!, the pro cougar, Latte crowd won that one, but we won the big one! Finally! Robert Dole has clinched up the GOP nomination!

And even though only 15% of eligible voters went to the polls, his anemic victory adds 165 Califonia delegates to his pie, which pushes his total, according to Tom Brokaw, to 1,198 delegates, which is clearly more than the 996 needed for nomination.

Pat!, it's over! Bob Dole won! His nomination is cemented in the driveway of time. And it's time for you to ride off in the sunset, waving your cowboy hat, Adios!

You had a lot of energy and a lot of spunk but the cowboy hat was where you went wrong. Your campaign nosed dived after you wore that hat. It made you look like Lou Costello, in Abbot and Costello Join the Rodeo.

So, Pat, drop out now and give Dole some peace.

You already ruined one President. You, and Colson and the other Watergate egg-er-on-ers. Your self serving twisted support of the negative, vindictive side of Nixon's personality, baited his trap. Your pony keg patriotism fueled his fall. His Quaker side was comatized. You stood on his shoulders waving the flag as the quick sand of lies you guys devised, pulled him down.

Then, Alone!, he carried his cross to San Clemente. The others, - Erlickman, Liddy, McGruder, all got jail time, and you got a Watergate Bride (Rosemary Wood's assistant), and a talk show on CNN. So, counterpoint your blessings, and let the cement dry.

Adios, giddyup, Go Pat Go,

PAT-GO

TREASURER

Mr. Lazlo Toth
PO Box 245
Fairfax CA 94978-0245

President Ed Rensi
McDonald's Co.
World Headquarters
Oak Brook, Illinois

May 15, 1996

Re: Arch DeLuxe

Dear President Rensi,

        Last week, I was among the first in line to try your
brand new sandwich, ARCH DELUXE. Unfortunately, I got it
"TO GO", so I didn't see it until I got home, and so I had
to drive all the way back to turn it back.

        You may be happy to know you've managed to brainwash
your employees to go along with your little trick, or maybe
they didn't understand what I was saying because I was
speaking ENGLISH. I'm sorry I don't know the word for
"ARCHES" in Spanish, but every AMERICAN in line agreed with
me when I showed it to them.
Yes, some smarty snot said, "the French fries are not from
France, but they call them French fries", but it's not the
same. Everyone knows that French fries are just called
that, but this sandwich is not even remotely shaped like an
ARCH — it's shaped round, like a regular hamburger.

        Mr. Renzi,- How can you call a sandwich ARCH DELUX
 and not have it shaped like an ARCH?".
Do you think people are not going to notice?
    Do you think people are so stupid that they don't know
what an arch looks like?

        You call yourselves "The Golden Arches". Why? Because
of those yellow curved pole things outside your restaurants,
the ARCHES! They are arched shaped — not round!
 If they were round, they would be called THE YELLOW WHEELS!
        But,they are NOT ROUND,they are ARCHED-SHAPED,- that's
why they are called ARCHES! So, now you deny it?

        If you sell a hamburger and call it "ARCHED", it makes
me think that your former failed burger, the "McLean Delux",
probaly wasn't "LEAN", and that the "Fish-O-Wich" is not
fish. I'm thinking maybe you call it "FISH-O-=WICH" because
you want people to WISH that it's fish.

    When are you going to stop doing this to people?

                        Lazlo Toth

McDonald's

McDONALD'S CORPORATION
OAK BROOK, ILLINOIS 60521
708/575-6198

July 15, 1996

Mr. Lazlo Toth
P.O. Box 245
Fairfax, CA 94978

Dear Mr. Toth:

Thanks for taking the time to write McDonald's and share your comments with
Ed Rensi about the name of the newest addition to our menu, the Arch Deluxe.
I'm glad I have this opportunity to respond to you.

As you can well imagine, we extensively test all aspects of a food product
(including its name) before we add it to our standard menu. As you recognized
in your letter, "arch" is synonymous with McDonald's. So calling our new
signature sandwich "Arch Deluxe" is like saying it's "McDonald's Deluxe."
During testing, customers told us they thought the name "Arch Deluxe" was a
good one... it described a sandwich that was uniquely McDonald's. Although the
shape of the sandwich didn't meet your expectations, we hope the taste
exceeded them!

Thanks again for sharing your viewpoint. We look forward to serving you under
the "Golden **Arch**es" for many years to come.

Sincerely.

Beth Petersohn
Office of the President
McDONALD'S CORPORATION

ARCH D**ELUXE**™

It's the burger with the grown up taste.™

TOTH Upholstery COMPANY
Specializing in Seat Covers for Miniature Cars
" No car is too small for seat covers."

LAZLO TOTH
Chairman

Representative Amo Houghton, R-N.Y
U.S. House of Representatives
Washington, D.C. 20515

Dear Congressman Houghton,

Your name was mentioned in the paper out here yesterday in the article about the mimimum wage going up to $4.75 per hour. You and other moderate republicans joined the House Democrats and were successful in defeating am attempt to pass an exemption for small business like mine.

"The center of the Republican party is back", Representative Amo Houghton, R-N.Y., exulted after the vote". That's what it said.

Well, that's great, Amo! Let the Upholsters and the Dry Cleaners and the Pet Shops pay the check, instead of the big companies with fancy skyscraper offices, and rat hole factories in places like the Phillipines. I could announce record profits too if my company was successful enough to be able to weasel around the minumum wage by taking advantage of poor people in third world countries.

Don't misunderstand me, I know that $4.75 is not a lot of money, and I think I'll be able to absorb the added labor cost you burden me with by just having Bambi and Randy work a few hours less each week, and using rubberbands for the miniature steering wheel covers, instead of stretch gause. But the big problem is that the buying power of that hourly wage is way less than ever before.

In the early 60's for an hours work at the minimum wage you could get eight McDonald's burgers. Today they have a new burger out there that's not even shaped like it's named, and how many of these McBovine sandwiches can you get for the present hourly minimum wage? I could tell you but instead I challenge you to get out in the real America and see how the standard of living for the average worker is going down! McWay down!

AND ONE REASON WHY? Not enough good paying jobs because American companies hire cheap foreign labor, and everytime the mimimum hourly rate goes up, there becomes a larger disparity between the wages of foreign workers and Americans.

That's why I would like you to consider sponsoring my plan that calls for American companies who make products abroad to raise the wages for foreign workers when wages are raised here at home.

Not only will THE HOUGHTON-TOTH BILL help keep more jobs in the U.S., and benefit our economy, but it will raise the standard of living in poorer, less fortunate nations, and at the same time take some of the load off the small upholstery type businesses and share it with the big corporations who give you guys big campaign contributions and buy you baseball tickets and free lunches.

Laźlo Toth

Lazlo H. Toth
Founder/Trainer

U.S. Rep. Gerald B. H. Solomon, R-NY
Chairman, House Rules Committee
Washington, D.C. 20515   June 6, 1996

Dear Congressman Solomon,

I read how you so gallantly defended the effort to repeal the assault weapons ban after Rep. Patrick Kennedy's speech in favor of keeping it.

You said, "My wife lives alone five days a week in a rural area in upstate New York.. She has a right to defend herself when I'm not there, son. And don't you ever forget it".

Mr. Solomon, not only does she have the right to defend herself when you're not there, she has the right to defend herself when she thinks you're not there, too.

What if she opens fire, spraying the area where she saw the hunched shadow, but instead of a beefy burglar out there by the Weber, it's a shadowy U.S. Congressman (you!), home a day early because you were fortunate enough to get a free lift on the Philip Morris jet that was taking Newt Gingrich up to Saratoga Springs to give the invocation at the Marlboro Menthol Light Emphysema Benefit Golf Tournament.

The line was busy, as usual, when you tried to call to tell her you left your house keys back in D.C., in your gym bag. So, you get home, and one minute you're looking for the hidden key underneath the garbage can, and next thing you know, you can't even be shown in an open casket because you look like Sonny Corleone after the Tattaglia family surprized him at the toll booth.

Now, the question is not, "Does she have a right to defend herself?", but, "Who is New York Governor Pataki going to name to serve out the remainder of your term?". You would probably say that your wife should be your replacement, that she has the right to defend your pro asssult weapon congressional seat, too. But, face it, she's got those darn manslaughter charges hanging over her head. And the trial may linger.

Yes!, she has a right to defend herself, but does she have the right to defend a garbage can that is in relatively little danger?

Yes!, accidents happen, but if a person "overreacts", is she <u>innocent</u> if she knowingly keeps and uses a weapon that is designed to over-react?

The right to defend yourself is one thing, but the need to do it with marine style assault weapons and turn people into one person swat teams, is something else.

And calling a U.S. Congressman, "son", is another thing altogether. It's insulting and demeaning, but worse, it's an affront to his assassinated Uncles, and shows disrespect for the sacrifices made by the family who's "son" he is.

Barks Not Bullets,

Lazlo Toth

Postmaster General Marvin Runyon
Main Post Office
Washington, D. C.

June 10, 1996

Dear Postmaster General Runyon,

Yesterday, President Clinton was in San Francisco for a
$100,000 per couple fund raiser at the home of Senator Diane
Feinstein. Gay demonstrators were picketing, angry over
Clinton's repudiation of "same sex" marriage. Personally,
I'm more concerned with his involvement in his "Same Scandal"
marriage, but this is not about Whitewater, that little rock
chicken will be home to roost soon enough.

Besides the demonstrators outside her home one could see
large U.S. Postal Service trucks, big as small moving vans,
about six of them, strategically parked in front of the the
house, hiding, better than a thick Bay fog, any glimpse of
the Highrollers who came to throw $100,000 checks into
President Bill's campaign wishing well.

General!, this "fund raiser", was a cheek to cheek,
wink wink, kiss my checkbook, disgusting event, put on by the
Buy A Wish Foundation, that raised a quick Three Million
Dollars for the Democratic National Committee.

Postmaster! Runyon!, why were Official U.S. Postal
Service trucks present at this obscene affair? Did you think
the donors were coming there to address envelopes?
Or, did the DNC rent the trucks? Or were they rented by
the Rose Law Firm, or by big donors like the Gallo Brothers,
Ernest and Julio, or their brother with the cheese? If so,
would you please inform this citizen how much they paid to
rent the trucks.

I hope it was top dollar, since you're losing the "One
Day Delivery" battle with Federal Express, and you haven't
had a hit stamp since Elvis Presley, and the only stamp that
can come close to matching that success is Jerry Garcia's,
and he still has nine more years to go until he qualifies for
stamphood.

BUT!, even if the Clinton people paid big bucks to rent
our trucks, should U.S. Postal vehicles be allowed to be
bumpered end to end, like drawn venetian blinds, cast in the
role of HEDGES, and used to block the sight of the crony
check-in-the-palm hand shakes and the cheese dip? Tell me
WHY!, Mr. Postmaster, these noble vans, with the proud Eagle
on their sides, were desecrated, and used to COVER UP the
voter's view of the polluted pond of politics.

And, so that you deliver your reply letter the sooner
the better, I enclose a 3 cent "A. W. Mellon", and a 29 cent
"Year of the Pigs".

Laszlo Toth

UNITED STATES
POSTAL SERVICE

June 17, 1996

XIAOMING DAI: Described as a Rim' real-estate developer, he w... Chinese national close to Beijing

JOHN HUANG: Already under scrutiny for soliciting improper foreign con-tributions for the DNC, he apparently brought Dai to the Feinstein dinner

David is an International Studies graduate stud...

Vice-Chair of the DNC. Pre... nomic Policy with t...

Mr. Lazlo Toth
P. O. Box 245
Fairfax, CA 94978-0245

Dear Mr. Toth:

The Postmaster General has asked me to respond to your letter of June 10, relative to a fund-raiser and alleged postal participation.

The Postal Service is a non-partisan, non-taxpayer, quasi-governmental organization. I can assure you that the Postal Service did not participate in the fund-raiser. The appearance of our vehicles can be easily explained.

From time to time, as the President tours the nation, the Secret Service will ask to utilize a number of larger empty postal vehicles for security purposes. I can assure you that this was the case last week in San Francisco.

Thank you for your concern and if I may be of further assistance, please contact me.

Best regards,

James H. Adams
Manager, Administration

Guess Who Came to Dinner

Last June the

The Flag & Torch Foundation

Office Postal Area 245   Fairfax, California 94978

**With the FLAG of hope in one hand,
and the TORCH of freedom in the other,
no hill is safe
from the charging legs of truth.**
                              - Lazlo Toth

September 25, 1996

TO: FUTURE PRESIDENT BOB DOLE
FROM: LAZLO TOTH / Freelance

Dear Bob,
     I just saw you on t.v (television) telling the press
that your cholesterol is lower than Clinton's. I think
you've got him on the run now!

     The best part of your acceptance speech was when you said
the Clinton administration was run by a bunch of kids who
"never grew up, never did anything real, never sacrificed,
never suffered or never even learned".
     But, Bob, they have learned a few things. They've learned
to JOG, drink "LATTE" coffee, and order pizza! You can throw
that in next time. And here's something elce I spun off the
pizza idea for you to use on him in the first debate:

> YOU: The only things those Domino pizza eating,
>   marijuana weed sucking spoiled brats who never
>   were even shot at, let alone wounded, know
>   about suffering is having to wait in the rain
>   by the Whitehouse gate for their pizzas and
>   Latte coffee to arrive. They probably think
>   Family Values means you save money if you
>   order the family size pizza.
>   I don't know why President Clinton doesn't just
>   put a Domino's Pizza parlor right in the
>   Whitehouse and save the American taxpayers the
>   money that the spoiled brats tip the Domino
>   delivery man. Fellow Americans, this is a
>   fact - The Clinton staff gets almost twice
>   as much pizza delivered to the White House in
>   <u>one day</u> than Maureen Reagan got when she was
>   living there in a WEEK! Check your logs,
>   Mr. President, let's set the record straight!

Here's another campaign slogan I'm giving you for FREE again.
You know, I wouldn't mind joining your staff and being paid.

From the Battlefields of Europe **To fighting traffic at Home**
BOB DOLE WAS THERE
Isn't it about time WE gave him something back?
BE THERE FOR BOB
He was there for You   *Lazlo Toth*

October 24, 1996

Mr. Lazlo Toth
P.O. Box 245
Fairfax, CA 94978

Dear Mr. Toth:

Thank you for your patience in awaiting our response to your
communication. The Dole/Kemp campaign is rolling along at
full speed, and with your help and the help of others in
Fairfax, we envision victory on November 5th!

Thank you for your suggestion. We appreciate your idea
because it provides perspective on what people across
America are thinking and how we can best communicate our
message of family values, less government, lower taxes,
better education and greater opportunities for everyone.

I hope Jack Kemp and I can count on your support on election
day.

Again, thank you for your comments.

Sincerely,

BOB DOLE

Authorized and paid for by Dole/Kemp '96, Robert E. Lighthizer, Treasurer

www.dolekemp96.org

THE HOLY FATHER POPE JOHN PAUL II's

1975 FORD ESCORT GL 4 DOOR SEDAN

Highest Bidder Wil Receive:

- A fine automobile
- Round trip tickets via Italia Airlines to Rome
- Oportunity to make check payable to The Pope John Paul II Foundation which is deductible
- Private mass in Pope's Chapel
- Presentation by the Pope of the Keys and Owner's manual
- Pope License Plate
- Places in the Vatican not normally shown

Buy Now, Pray Later

In Auburn, Ind., Kruse International is auctioning off a 1975 Ford Escort that was driven by Pope **John Paul II** when he was Cardinal **Karol Wojtyla**.

KNIGHTS
of
SERRA

Pope John Paul II
Vatican City, Vatican

Your Holiness,

My reading continues to drift towards astronomy, and I was wondering if the church has a positon on the possibility of the existence of a "Mirror Planet" of Earth.

Some astronomers say there exists a planet <u>exactly</u> like earth, but we can't see it because it's blocked from us by the Sun.
It's on the exact other side of the sun from us.

Holiness, IF there is such a thing as a MIRROR planet of Earth, how can we be sure that we're the REAL Earth, and not the mirror? And if there is a Pope on that planet, and he looks EXACTLY like you, is he infallable, too? — or does he just THINK he is?
That's my main question.

Also, when you had your appendix out yesterday, would you mind telling me what they did with it? Do they dispose of a Papal appendix just as they would an ordinary human's, or are special precautions taken? Perhaps it's not just discarded, but kept in a safe place until some kind of corporal reunion takes place with the remaining future remains. Or, perhaps it's already being treated as a Relic, and was immediately FED EX'ed on ice to some Cathedral in Krakow.

ANYWAY, on Labor Day, in Indiana, they raffled off the 1975 Ford Escort you drove when you were a Cardinal for one hundred and two thousand dollars. <u>$102,000</u>! Think what a deserving non profit organization could get for your appendix! I know it hasn't been working for you very well, but I bet it's in better shape than your old Escort! That's a funny joke I send to you!.
But seriously, IF you wouldn't mind your appendix being sent abroad to be raffled off, my fellow Knights and I would use the proceeds to support our stuggle to obtain Sainthood for Father Serra.

How much longer must we wait?   *Lazlo Toth*

FATHER SERRA SAINTHOOD NOW!

The Flag & Torch Foundation

WHERE HOPE IS STILL AN OPTION.
November 5, 1996 / Election Day

Senator Bob Dole
c/o The Watergate Apartments
Washington, D.C.

Lazlo Toth
P.O. Box 245
Fairfax
California 94978

Dear Bob,

    I got your letter too late! I went down to Mexico and I just got back yesterday. So, I want you to know from the top that I'm a little testy having to leave sunny, Mexico, in order to fulfill my duties and vote and give back something to Bob Dole, a man who keeps his word and only gave and never took - Bob Dole! That's you! Stand!

    You were good in the second debate but you shouldn't have referred to the American people as "the pipeline", and your program for the future as "a good package". Those catchy thoughts would have been warmly humanized if I was overseeing your campaign, but it's late now!

    Yes!, Bob, one gets a little upset when they come up with FREE ideas and suggestions and the Dole camp ignores his letters and makes him feel like going to Mexico to celebrate the day of the dead.

    But Bob, I don't know what I could have done more. It does not look good. Clinton is way ahead. I think our only chance now is to beg people to at least not vote against you, they owe you that!

    This is all I could come up with. I think it's too late now, but maybe you can use it next time.

<u>Do BOB DOLE</u>, a man who was
always there for you <u>A Favor</u>
STAY HOME ON ELECTION DAY
Dole was there for you, Don't be there for Him.
We owe him that much!
BURROW FOR BOB

Lazlo

Comeblow thehorns
of the
NEW Year
1997

TO: President Bill Clinton, c/o The White House.
FROM: Lazlo Toth, Poet Laureate Applicant - second notice.

RE: President William Jefferson Clinton
and V. P. Albert Forrest Gore III ReInauguration 1997

I am writing again so soon because I have not heard a word, not even a Christmas card back, regarding my Hoilday greetings to you, asking if you would consider me to be the Poet Laureate for your second inauguration, instead of Myra Angelou, who I understand has deceided to quit just like Leon Panetta.

Mr. President, there are many great poets in America, some who write with great passion, others with dazzling decriptions and unique styles, but I feel you will choose the next Poet Laureate from one of three categories:

1. Poets who donated money to your re-election campaign.
2. Poets who donated to your reinaruguraltion fund.
3. Poets who donated money to your re-election campaign, and to your reinauguration fund.

Mr. President, with this small donation to help fund your second inauguration gala, I proudly baptise myself into category number two, and promise, if chosen, to be the best Poet Laureate this country has ever had. I am willing to write up to three poems a day for the duration of my term, and after the government is done with them, I will donate all proceeds from my poems to a Fund to help Poets with spelling problems and puntuation disorders, except for those poems which refer directly to you or to your legal matters, in which case the proceeds will be sent directly to your team of lawyers. Through gestures such as these, I hope to be remembered as the first Team Player Poet Laureate.

One question: I was wondering - Would be all right, at the reInauguration, for me to have my poem on cue-cards?
Also, do I need boots? I have gloves, but I don't own winter boots. I just wondered what you thought the odds for snow were, if I would need them or not.

Enc: $1 U.S.

Lazlo Toth

THE WHITE HOUSE

WASHINGTON

February 21, 1997

Mr. Lazlo Toth
Post Office Box 245
Fairfax, California 94930

Dear Mr. Toth:

Thank you for your kind offer.

Although the President is unable to accept your services, on his behalf I want to extend gratitude for the spirit of generosity and cooperation that prompted your offer.

President Clinton appreciates your support.

Sincerely,

James A. Dorskind
Special Assistant to the President
Director of Correspondence and
Presidential Messages

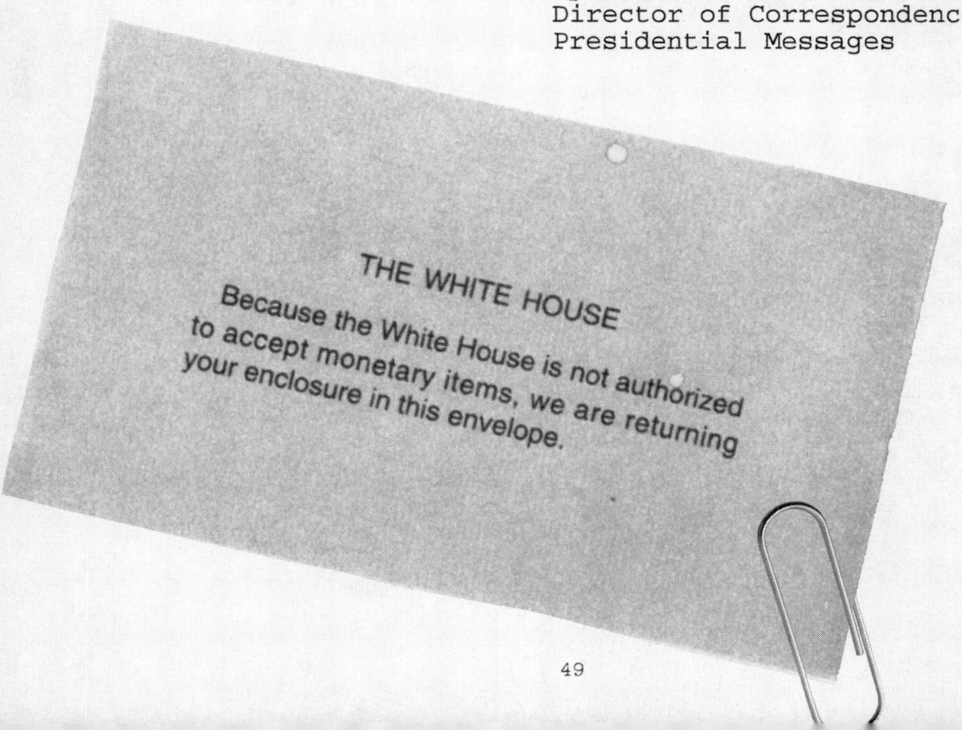

THE WHITE HOUSE
Because the White House is not authorized
to accept monetary items, we are returning
your enclosure in this envelope.

THE RITZ

1-1 7-9 7

Sarah "Lady Fergie" Ferguson, F.P.
c/o Weight Watchers International
175 CrossWays Park West
Woodbury, ny 11797

Dear Former Princess Ferguson,

    My dictionary does not list the proper form of address
for a former member-in-law of monarchy, so I hope I am not
out of line by referring to you as "Former Princess", which I
feel more comfortable with then "Former Lady", which sounds
as though you were found guilty of doing something un-lady-
like, when all you did was bail out of a marriage made
impossible by a Mother-in-law-Dearest, who wants you to live
in a barn, and acts like she's the Queen Bee, which she is.

    Well, I hope Her Highness was watching CNN today like I
was, and she saw how you knocked everybody's socks off during
that press conference with your remarks about your former
eating habits and partners.

    It just goes to show that all that royal training has
paid off, and that your weight gain has come home to roost in
the form of a paycheck of one million dollars a year with all
expenses paid by one of the leading intergloberated firms in
the health related arena.
I congradulate you on being named the new Weight WatchersI
spokesperson, and I care what the Queen Windsor thinks about
it about as much as I care about Englich Toffee.

                    Send me your picture, I will
                      put it on my refrigerator,

                  Pazlo Toth

    p.s.
    I hate to admit it, but I'm
    your Mother-in-law's distant cousin.
    But not ~~the~~ on the
    Hapsberg (Bleeder)
    (Bad Hair)
    side.

**FERGIE'S FUMING!
Queen wants her
to live in a barn**

Fergie flew into a royal rage when Queen Elizabeth offered her a new home — a horse barn!

5th March 1997

Dear Lazlo,

The Duchess of York (not Sarah Lady Fergie Ferguson) has passed your letter to me.

The Duchess was very touched that you took the time and trouble to write to her but she is very sorry to have to disappoint you as she is unable to send any photographs or autographs.

The Duchess has asked me to send you her good wishes.

Yours sincerely,
Hilary Bett

Miss Hilary Bett
Personal Secretary to The Duches of York

Lazlo Toth Esq.

Lazlo Toth
Post Office Box 245
Fairfax, California 94978

February 28, 1997

James A. Dorskind
Director of Special Correspondence to the President
The White House
Washington

Dear Special Director Dorskind,

   I was quite shocked when I received your letter. I read that The White House was returning "suspects'" money, but I never thought my contribution would be included among them.
   I think there has been a major misunderstanding.
   All I wanted to do was contribute to the President's Re-inaugruration Gala, and just because I made my contribution around the same time as when I was under consideration for an important Federal Poetry Position, people read ineuendo things into it.

   Yes!, I admit I wanted to be the Poet Laureate! Who wouldn't? But my donation was in no way linked to my being chosen, and as solid proof, I submit to you the fact that the job instead went to a poet from Arkansas, and he was no William Whitman Longfellow, if you know what I mean. Just about everybody I know agrees with me that I would have done much better.
   I think the mistake I made was mentioning that I wanted to have my poem on cue-cards. I think it was the added cue-card, magic marker expense, that tilted the scales towards the donor-poet from the President's home state. (Category #3)

   But what did I do that was so wrong, so bad!, to have my donation sent back to me in a small, sealed manila envelope, STAMPED, like it contained "evidence", - like some hair follicle found on a pillow case that's being sent to a lab for further testing.

   Mr. Dorrskind, I believe if I accept back my donation, it may be perceived by some as a sign of GUILT, and so I think it's wise for all concerned, if you would reconsider my small contribution, and let it join, with honor, the millions of others that were accepted to participate in the Re-Inauguaration Gala, which was re-markably Gala in my opinion. I more than got my dollar's worth!, plus I was able to tape it on my neighbors VCR, and some day I hope to look at again, if they don't record something over it and damage the evidence.

   encl: one small Brown envelope   Laszlo Toth

THE WHITE HOUSE
WASHINGTON

WASHINGTON, DC 200
PM
14 MAY
1997

50th Anniver
Coast Guard
1941
USA 32

Mr. Lazlo Toth
Post Office Box 245
Fairfax, CA 94930

94978-0245

THE WHITE HOUSE

Because the White House is not authorized
to accept monetary items, we are returning
your enclosure in this envelope.

March 3, 1997

Bob Nugent
President - Jack In The Box Restaurants
C/O Foodmaker
9330 Balboa Ave
San Diego, CA 92123

LAZLO TOTH
Post Office Box 245, Fairfax, California 94978

Dear Mr. President Nugent,

I am writing concerning a commercial where your guy with the big ping pong ball on his head - JACK? - is talking into the intercom outside the gates of a southern mansion that resembles a mausoleum, trying to deliver a Jack-in-the-Box spicy chicken sandwich to "The Colonel", and he wants to talk to him, "Founder to Founder".

Of course, the reference is to Colonel Harland Sanders, the founder of Kentucky Fried Chicken, a company who not long ago chose to change its name to "KFC". Why did the current management abandon the name bestowed upon it over 40 years ago by its heroic founder and adopt three consonants of the alphabet in its stead? Why? Because the word FRIED "tested negative" in research done with "focus groups"! YES!, the name of a company, a name that represents one of the supreme success stories in American cuisine history, is overthrown!, not by a franchise from a foreign shore, or not even as a result of negative publicity deriving from the effects of a chicken coop borne Virus, but by the whims of RESEARCH, the slippery nephew of GREED.

Now the fancy executives at "KFC" have to live with their short sighted decision to stab their Founder-Father in the back, and biting the bread crumb covered hand of the man who came up with the secret blend of herbs and spices that changed the eating habits of a nation and made it possible for all of them to get finger-lickin' filthy rich. I don't want to be judgemental, but I know I don't want to be them come Judgement Day. And I don't want to be you either! Because, it's not nice to make fun of the dead!

Mr. President, Colonel Sanders has been "on the night shift" for over twenty years. So, is your commercial's pathetic attempt at humor designed solely to bring sorrow to a competitors family and estate, or is it part of some kind of a greater business tactic meant to enhanse your desperate ping pong head image by demeaning the legendary leader in the fast chicken field? Do you think you will win points with the American public by insulting a man who already has been posthumously tared and feathered by his own company?

<u>Here's an idea for you:</u>
Put your ping pong brain mascot in a small boat and have him go out livevestless in the open sea to talk to the fish, "Founder to Flounder", and LET THE COLONEL REST IN PEACE!

A m e n,

Laylo Toth

A Division of
Foodmaker, Inc.
9330 Balboa Avenue
San Diego, CA 92123-1516
619/571-2121

June 9, 1997

Mr. Lazlo Toth
P.O. Box #245
Fairfax, CA 94978

Dear Lazlo:

Thank you for taking the time to contact us at JACK IN THE BOX
with your comments regarding our Spicy Crispy Chicken Sandwich
commercial. I have forwarded your comments to our Marketing
Communications Department. This is the department responsible
for our television and radio advertising.

Again, thank you for taking the time to write to us. I have
enclosed some coupons for your use at one of our restaurants. I
hope you enjoy your next visit to JACK IN THE BOX.

Sincerely,

Karen Woodard

Karen Woodard
Guest Support Representative
Guest Support Team

gt10922

Lazlo Toth
Post Office Box 245
Fairfax, California 94978

March 4, 1997

To: Albert Forrest Gore Jr.
Vice President of the United States of America, Washington.
FROM: Lazlo Toth
Registered voter, State of California, Fairfax.

RE: Telephone Solicitations Made From Your Office:

It was a mistake today when you went before the Press and said,
"I didn't do anything wrong, and I won't do it again".
You sounded like the guy who was caught selling bad fish who
said, "I didn't know the pond was polluted, I told people not to eat
more than one per week".

But, Mr. Vice President, even if you strong armed contributors,
like some say, this unfortunate turn of events is not your fault.
The system is at fault!
The problem is that the office of Vice President, officially, has
hardly anything to do. If the President likes you, he can give you
important assignments and enhance your image and prestige.
If he doesn't like you, or if you choose not to be one of his"team
players", you'll spend the next four years walking around the halls
of the Whitehouse feeling like a ham at a Bar Mitzvah.

So, what else can you do? When you're the understudy for <u>Annie</u>,
you don't want poeple going around satyying you don't have
chemistry with Daddy Warbucks! So, you go to a few $10,000 a plate
Spaghetti Dinners in the bacement of Buddist Temples. You help the
President change the sheets in the Lincoln bedroom. And, Yes!, you
make a few phone calls to high roller donor friends and friends of
friends.
But, Vice President, Gore, don't be down on yourself:
<u>It's a Proven Fact</u>:
<u>If a person talks on the phone long</u>
<u>enough, he's going to get into trouble.</u>

So, to cheer you up, come what may, I want to make an early
contribution to your future Presidential campaign. And!, I would
like be the First! to make another contribution to the campaign after
that one.

Lazlo Toth

Enclosed: $2 CASH.
One for "<u>GORE in 2000</u>", and One for "<u>More Gore in 2004</u>".

OFFICE OF THE VICE PRESIDENT
WASHINGTON

May 28, 1997

Mr. Lazlo Toth
P. O. Box 245
Fairfax, California   94978-0245

Dear Mr. Toth:

    Your message to the Vice President concerning recent reports about
his fundraising activities in the last election has been received in this
office, and I welcome the opportunity to respond to you.

    During the election, the Vice President took a leadership role in
the effort to ensure the reelection of President Clinton and himself and
the continuation of the very positive and successful policies that this
Administration has implemented. Throughout his career in public office,
Vice President Gore has adhered to the highest standards of personal and
professional conduct. The 1996 campaign was no exception.

    Since your comments reflect a specific concern about the
Vice President's calls from the White House, I have taken the liberty of
enclosing for your review a recent "op-ed" piece relating to this matter
from the New York Times.

    Beyond all of this, however, lies a greater question involving the
need for comprehensive and substantive campaign finance reform.
Vice President Gore has supported reform since his earliest days in
Congress, where he introduced bills to provide for complete public
financing of elections and to provide free television time on the public
airwaves for national candidates.

    Likewise, since taking office, the President and the Vice President
have been strong proponents of campaign finance reform legislation. A
bipartisan bill, sponsored by Senators McCain and Feingold, has been
introduced in the Congress. The President has endorsed it, is working
actively to pass it, and has pledged to sign it. If you are concerned
about the current system of financing the nation's political campaigns, I
encourage you to contact your representatives in Congress and urge them
to support reform legislation this year.

Sincerely,

Bill Mason

Bill Mason
Director of Correspondence
   for the Vice President

March 7, 1997

Janet Reno
Attorney General
Department of Justice
Washington, D.C.

Lazlo Toth
Post Office Box 245
Fairfax, California 94978

Dear Attorney General,

I agree with you that there is no need to appoint a Special Prosecutor to investigate the recent domestic and foreign contribution irregularities made to the Clinton-Gore campaign.

Our country does not need another Watergate. Especially if innocent people such as innocent! potential poet nominees have to be dragged into it.

<u>One question:</u>
A few days ago, when the Vice President (Gore) went before the press to deny any wrong doings, he kept saying (seven times! he said it!), that his lawyer told him to say, "there is no controlling legal authority that says that any of these activities violated any law".

I was wondering: IF, just IF, the vice president made solicitatious telephone calls from his official Vice Presidential office in the Whitehouse to people in boats outside the seventeen mile limit, would the U.S. Coast Guard have controlling legal authority over such a situation since the phone call originated within the continental U.S.?

Just wondering for my own information,

Lazlo Toth

Lazlo Toth

U. S. Department of Justice

Criminal Division

Washington, D.C. 20530

July 1, 1998

Mr. Lazio Toth
P.O. Box 245
Fairfax, California 94978

Dear Mr. Toth:

Thank you for your letter to the Attorney General. She has asked me to respond to you on her behalf regarding the Department of Justice's investigation of possible violations of campaign finance law in the last election cycle.

Your letter raises several specific issues regarding the criminal investigation being conducted by the Department into campaign finance allegations. Unfortunately, we are limited in the response we can make since the Department cannot comment on the specifics of the ongoing criminal investigation that we are conducting into allegations of possible violations of campaign finance laws.

I wish to reassure you, however, that the Department is conducting a vigorous and comprehensive investigation, and will follow the facts wherever they may lead. Furthermore, the Attorney General has made clear that she will continue to make her decisions based solely on those facts and on the law.

In order to pursue this investigation, the Attorney General has established a task force with more than 120 members, including senior prosecutors and FBI agents. The task force's work has not been halted by the Attorney General's previous conclusions that there was no basis for seeking an independent counsel. As the Attorney General explained, a "decision not to ask for an independent counsel does not mean that a person has been exonerated or that the work of the campaign finance task force has ended." To the contrary, the Attorney General stated, the Department "will continue to vigorously investigate all allegations of illegal activity." Furthermore, should the facts developed by the task force make it appropriate to initiate further preliminary investigations under the Independent Counsel Act, the Attorney General will not hesitate to do so.

The Attorney General appreciates the time and effort you took to write to share your point of view. We hope that this response addresses some of your concerns.

Sincerely,

Betsy L. Pond

Betsy L. Pond
Executive Office

March 9
1 9 9 7

Senator Diane Feinstein
U.S. Senate
Washington, D.C.

LAZLO TOTH
Post Office Box 245, Fairfax, California 94978

Dear Senator Feinstein,

I was appalled to read that many of the wild horses put up for adoption in the Bureau of Land Management's "Adopt-a Horse" Program, end up in slaughter houses, and that "more than 200 bureau employees who have adopted 600 wild horses now can't account for their whereabouts". It sounds like the same thing is happening to our wild horses as what happened to Jimmy Hoffa. One minute you're out running in the open range or walking in the parking lot of some suburban Detroit restaurant, and next thing you know, you're adopted by Alpo.

Also, in today's Sunday Examiner, the headline say's you were one of six members of congress that was targeted by China to receive illegal campaign contributions funneled through foreign corporations, and it hit me like a bag of rice, that there might have been foreign funnelers among the group that President Clinton brought over to your house for his post-Presidio $100,000 a plate fund raiser last summer.

I'm not sure of the exact date, (check June 9th, 1996), but I remember clearly it was foggy, and because of the official U.S. Postal Service trucks that were parked bumper to bumper in front of your house to protect our President, the press could not see who else (besides the trucks) was there.

So, I was just thinking that maybe it might be wise for you to get the guest lists from the Democtatic National Committee, and let the press know if any foreigners were there and if you saw any of them give a check or cash, a bond, or any kind of monetary item to the President while he was schmoozing in your home. From what we've been reading lately, you're lucky he didn't invite some of his special donor friends to sleep over. For all you know, some Koreans could still be camped out in your attic.

Senator, I hope that you will address these issues as soon as possible and do the right thing for the good of the Citizens and Horses who live in the state and territory you cover.

Lazlo Toth

STAND BY OUR FLAG!

Lazlo Toth

DIANNE FEINSTEIN
CALIFORNIA

United States Senate
WASHINGTON, DC 20510-0504

April 24, 1997

Mr. Lazlo Toth
PO Box 245
Fairfax, California 94978

Dear Mr. Toth:

Thank you for contacting me concerning the Adopt-a-Horse-or-Burro program administered by the Bureau of Land Management (BLM). I appreciate hearing from you on this important issue.

The Wild Free-Roaming Horse and Burro Act was passed in 1971 to protect wild horses and burros on western public lands. This act provides criminal penalties for individuals who remove, kill, harass, or sell federally protected wild horses or burros. It also directs the BLM to manage the herds of wild horses and burros in order to protect the ecological integrity of federal rangelands and ensure the long-term survival of the animals. Currently, about 42,000 wild horses and burros in ten western states are protected by this act.

The primary method used by the BLM to remove healthy wild horses and burros from overpopulated areas is the Adopt-a-Horse-or-Burro Program. Under this program, individuals may adopt healthy animals for a fee of $125. After one year of providing humane care, adopters may receive title to their horse or burro.

I understand your concern about recent reports that animals adopted under this program have been sold to slaughterhouses. The BLM is currently investigating this matter and reviewing its adoption procedures to determine what changes are necessary to protect these animals from abuse. Please know that I am also monitoring this situation carefully, and I will certainly keep your concerns in mind if the Senate takes any action to address this issue.

Again, thank you for contacting me. I am working hard to represent California in the Senate, and I hope you will feel free to contact me again in the future on any other issue of concern to you. If you have any specific questions or comments on this issue, please call Dave Chadwick in my Washington, D.C. office at

(202) 224-3841.

With warmest personal regards.

Sincerely yours,

Dianne Feinstein

RADIO ONE WATT

We Changed Out Format!
No more, "The Lonely One" - Now we're,

"WATT ONE WANTS!"

P.O. Box 245   Fairfax, California   94978

Lazlo Toth
Assistant Station Manager

Dole Takes a Job As Washington Lawyer

Washington — Bob Dole, who said last May when he quit the Senate that he had "nowhere to go but the White House or home," has found a third alternative — a job as a Washington lawyer.

The defeated Republican presidential candidate, who has been wooed by several major Washington law firms, agreed yesterday to join Verner, Liipfert, Bernhard, McPherson & Hand, which is stocked with several heavy-hitting Democrats. Dole will be offering "strategic advice" on public-policy issues to the firm's long roster of clients, which includes approximately 90 Fortune 500 companies.

Former Hon. Senator Bob Dole
Verner, Liipfert, Bernhard, McPherson & Hand
901 15th Street NW
Washington, D.C.

April 19, 1997

Dear Bob,

Boy, have you been in the news lately! Here's a story about your new job that I clipped out of the paper a few days ago, and you were in the paper again today about how you're going to give a $300,000 loan to Neut Gringrich. I was going to send that article, too, but I misplaced my scissors.

I'll be honest, I was getting a little irritated about you taking so long to get back to me about the interview, and I should have realized you were out job hunting. I hope VLBM&H has good benefits and you'll be able to stop sponging off your wifes' Red Cross "family" coverage, and that that insurance money can be freed up to help flood victims.

Things have changed a little here at the station, but for now, I'm still able to honor my offer to you of 10 minutes of air time and an unlimited number of plugs (up to four) for any product or corporation you want to mention. But!, the new station manager, Debbie, insists that if it's a foreign corporation you're plugging, you'll have to sign a form that states that the Corporation hasn't tried to influence the U.S. electoral system within the last 18 months to the best of your knowledge.

Bob, I can't say how wonderful it was of you to bail out Neut. It reminded me of when Mr. Grant loaned money to Ted Baxter on The Mary Tyler Moore Show. And just like Lou Grant, you played it down, but everybody knows now that you're a real softy and to this I say, "Skoal!". Once someone went to toast drinks with Dean Martin and they said, "Skoal!", and Dino said, "Sure skoal, it's got ice in it!" I'll bet people hit on him a lot for loans, too.

But, Bob, excuse me, but it's just not right that you should have the burden of carrying a $300,000 loan this late in your game plan. So, here enclosed, find $1 CASH to partially reimburse your sacrifice, and to show support of your decision to support the Speaker.

This Dollar Bill (L48417631E) will be remembered as the starter dough of an organization I have christened, Ethics Penalty Patriot Partners. with a goal of enlisting 299,999 other patriots, who will each be instructed to send One Dollar to your office, with the understanding that once the $300,000 reimbursement level has been reached, the membership will be closed, no further loans accepted, no exceptions.

So, sign where I put the arrow, and then all you've got to do is get a physical exam from a licensed physician, and it's a DONE DEAL.

Lazlo Toth

R1W

Ethics Penalty Patriot Partners

A partially non-partisan totally volunteer Patrol of Partners
dedicated to sharing an unjust Penalty in a just manner.

Contract

On this day: **April 19, 1997**

Be it here known that:

Name: **Ethics Penalty Patriots** (Lender)
Lazlo Toth, Founding Partner,
plus 299,999 other future Partner/Investors,

Hereby promise to share the financial responsibilities of the
unjust penalty laid on Neut Gringrich, the Speaker of the United
States House Representatives, with:

Name: **Robert (Bob) Dole** (Borrower)
Employer: Verner, Liipfert, Bernhard, McPherson & Hand
Job: Lawyer

We herewith offer to loan Mr. Bob Dole the same number of
dollars and the same lenient terms he offered Speaker Gringrich.

<u>The loan amount shall be</u>: **$300,000**
$1 each from 300,000 patriots.

<u>The interest rate shall be</u>: **10%**, calculated on an annual basis,
over an eight year period, with principal and all accrued interest
due and payable on: **April 19, 2005,**

At which time Mr. Gringrich will owe Mr. Dole
the amount of: **$640,000**
And Mr. Dole will owe Mr. Toth
(And the other 299,999 Ethics Penalty Parners)
the amount of: **$ 2.03 Each**.

SIGN
HERE

Lazlo Toth, for EPPP (Lender)

Robert "Bob" Dole, (Borrower)

TOTHWORKS
P.o.BoX245FairFax,CaliFornia
9 4 9 7 8
23. 4. 9 7

Lazlo Toth
Chairman

Hon. Speaker Neut Grinrich
United States House of Reprsenatives
Washington, D.C.   20515

Dear Neut,
    It was a smart move on your part to make up with Bob
Dole and accept his offer to loan you money. As Art Agnos,
the former Mayor of San Francisco once said, "If I stopped
talking to everyone who ever stabbed me in the back, I
wouldn't have any friends".

    Neut, I have an idea for a movie and I want to get a go
ahead from you before I present it to Mr. Joe Pesce.
    I know you probably would prefer someone like Nick
Nolte or Rod Stieger to play yourself in a movie, but I
understand Mr. Steiger has already gotten wind of this
project, and will to be out of the country until we're done
shooting it. And as for Nick Nolte, it looks like he is
going to be unavailable because Duvall is passing on the
Rostenkowski project (<u>Daniel My Brother</u>), and Nolte is the
directors first second choice.

    But, for all we know, the whole thing may fall apart.
Rostenkowski is turning into a real prima-donna. He's
insisting that Bobby Vinton does the soundtrack, and they say
Elton John refuses to give permission to use the title song
if Vinton has any involvement whatsoever, so who knows.

    Speaker, I've done all this work on spec, and I don't
want to go into a litany about my nut, all I know is that
this movie is a sure thing blockbuster, IF it can only make
it to the screen. The problem is keeping the project afloat
while were fishing for financing. If you have any family or
friends, or business associates even, who would like to get
in at the ground floor, let me know their names and address
and I'll prospectus them with a fairly flexible story summary
and a rough ballpark budget estimate. Then, if they're still
interested after that, I can meet with them personally.
    <u>TOTHWORKS STUDIOS</u> are headquartered about 25 miles
NORTH of the Golden Gate Bridge, and just a few minutes
SOUTH of George Lucas' SKYWALKER RANCH, but we're doing a
lot of construction here on the lot , getting the place in
shape for the millinium, and there's a lot of dust around, so
I think it would be better if I flew to meet with your people
at your office in D.C.

    You can reimburse my travel costs, or I can coordinate
flights and hotel reservations with your secretary. The main
thing now is to keep a positive attitude!
    This movie could be bigger than <u>The People vs. Larry Flynt</u>!

Lazlo Toth

TOTHWORKS!

Meet Neut Gringrish
Year: 2005

He Owes Bob Dole
$625,000.

CASH.

Dole would absolve
the Debt ...
BUT!,
Dole's got
Debts of his Own.
He owes
300,000 Americans
$2.06.

Cash.

Each.

Neut knows what
he has to do.

JOE PESCI
300,000 HEADS
- IN A -
DUFFEL BAG.

BOB DOLE
as Himself

Andi McDowell
as Liddy Dole

COMING!

Senator Bob Dole

May 9, 1997

Dear Mr. Toth:

Thanks for your letter and for the $1.00. Unfortunately, I am unable to accept this money and your offer of assistance. I am returning the one dollar bill as it would violate the terms of the agreement.

The Speaker came to the conclusion that it was simply wrong to ask the taxpayers to pay for an investigation and I applaud his decision to pay with personal funds.

For that reason and many more, Newt is a friend and I am pleased that I can be of assistance.

I am looking forward to my new challenges with Verner, Liipfert, Bernhard, McPherson and Hand.

Sincerely,

BOB DOLE

Mr. Lazlo Toth
Assistant Station Manager
RADIO ONE WATT
P.O. Box 245
Fairfax, California 94978

The Queen of England
Her Highness Elizabeth Windsor (Head)
c/o Buckingham Palace
London, England

4 -5- 97
L a z l o T o t h
P. O .B. 2 4 5
Fairfax, California
9 4 9 7 8 U S A

Dear Queen Elizabeth,

I think it's wonderful you made Paul McCartney a Knight, but I don't think it was very nice of you to bestow it to him on the same day you also bestowed some other title of honor on Joan Collins. It would be like you going to be honored at some fancy dinner, and finding out Emelda Marcos was being honored, too. It would take a little wind out of your balloon, am I right?

But!, in spite of the unfortunate linkage, I'm glad you did it. Paul McCartney should have been made a Knight years ago, in my opinion. Frankly, I don't know what took you so long.

But, Highness, one question: - I know it's probably none of my business, I'm just an American, but, -<u>Why not the other Beatles, too?</u>

I was thinking maybe you didn't make John Lennon a Knight because there's some kind of rule that say's a person can't be made a Knight postumously. But, if that's the rule, you can change it, - you're the Queen! Who's going to complain, the Duke of Earl?

So, more most likely, I figure you probably have some kind of a festering royal vendetta against John Lennon. Maybe you're still mad about that song about "How many holes there are in Albert Hall". That's probably a building that your family owns, am I right?

Or, I was thinking, maybe you were threatened when he sang, "Imagine no Religion", and that you feared next he would say "Imagine no Royalty", or, "Imagine the Queen of England having to pay Property Taxes ". But, you should let bygones be bygones. He paid the ultimate price for his vision and freedom of mind, and he sure doesn't need to be postumously snubbed for being ahead of his time at this late date.

And how about Ringo Starr and George Harrison? What's your excuse for not Knighting them? Did you think <u>Hold On Boogaloo</u> was meant to boost the morale of freedom fighters in Ireland? Do you think <u>My Sweet Lord </u>sounds too much like <u>Hail Britainia</u> ?

From this side of the pond, Highness, your divisive, Yokoish actions, makes one wonder if you are truly a Paul McCartney and a Beatles fan, or just a control freak and trouble maker, and that Kieth Richards, as well as all the Hermits, are next in line to be royally snubbed over, when you Knight up Herman and Mick Jagger next.

Lazlo Toth

A Non-Profit Division of
THE KNIGHTS OF SERRA
LAZLO TOTH
President-Elect

Lady Cherie Blair
Prime Spouce
10 Downing Street
London, England

May 9, 1997

Dear Madame Cherie,

I can't tell you how relieved a lot of us Yanks were when we read that you said you think cats are unhygienic. What with all the hoopla over certain English people (I'm not metioning any names) being forced to live in unhygenic conditions (barn), just because her Mother-in-law is carrying a grudge, it's a relief to know not all English people are unaware of the hazards of the millions of microscopic germs carried on a daily basis by members of the Feline (cat) and Equestrian (horse) communities, and 10 Downey Street without a resident cat (Humphrey), will certainly not make the place any less hygenic, that's for sure.

As you, your children and newly elected Prime Minister husband begin your stay in the famous residence, I suggest you Check-Mate your Pro Cat (Tory) critics in the press by adding a member of the Canine branch of the animal kingdom to your family.

I have in my ward an elderly Golden Retriever, her name - MAUREEN, and I would be willing to have her shipped to you, at our expense, FREE of charge. Aside from a minor hearing disorder, she is in fairly good health for her age (16), and still loves her long naps and mashed snacks.

IF the new Second Family of England were to adopt an elderly dog from abroad, your husband's newly in power Labour party would firmly re-establish the special bond that existed between our countries in the days of Reagan and Thrasher, and the positive world-wide attention this story will generate will more than make up for the negative press you received about Humphrey the cat being booted.

Say "YES!", and you not only give Maureeen a new home, but you will take the burden of upkeep of one old dog, who still has a big appetite, off the shoulders of an organization that needs all the help it can get. How people who make the morally right decison to put a dog in an elderly boarding residence, but then fail to maintain the financial obligations for their former best friend's upkeep, is more than a matter of manners and money, but more a matter of Honesty and Justice, and one on which the very fabrics of western civilization could begin to unleash. That's why a gesture such as yours, an adoption with high visability potential, is so important for our cause.

On Maureen's behalf,

Laylo Toth

1O DOWNING STREET
LONDON SW1A 2AA

From the Office of Cherie Booth QC   13 August 1997

Mr Lazo Tosh
Dog Heaven
Post Office Box 245
Fairfax
California
USA

Dear Mr Tosh

I am writing on behalf of Cherie Booth QC to thank you for your recent letter.
Your comments have been noted.

Yours sincerely

Roz Preston
Assistant to Cherie Booth QC

LAZLO TOTH
THE STATE OF CALIFORNIA

Lazlo Toth
Post Office Box 245
Fairfax, California 94978

CHAIRMAN / Poetry   Division
Citizen's Oversight Committee

Defense Secretary William Cohen
Department of Defense
Washington, D.C.

THANKSGIVING DAY
11-27-97

Dear Secretary Cohen,

I believe that as a Poet Laureate Alumnus (Nominee Applicant), I have the right to be considered for burial at Arlington National Cemetery. Obviously, since I am alive at present, I am not ready yet (to be buried), but I am taking this opportunity to inquire, as when the time comes, I might be caught off guard, and have missed the opportunity to apply. Sometimes, in the death arena, we are smashed, zinged, or swooped away without proper warning, and letters we wished we had written, such as this request for an application to a National cemetery, go unanswered since they were never executed, - hense this missive to you.

But first, let's get something straight - In the article about the Clinton administration pulling strings, and selling plots to some H.R.D.C's (High Roller Democrat Contributors), I see that you're internmenting some bodies in the same grave as a relative who has already beem D&B'd (Dead and Buried) there previously. This I do not want! And, excuse me if I'm wrong, but I don't think it's asking too much for a person to want his own grave! To me, it's like having fresh sheets on the bed when you go to a motel or a B&B (Bed and Breakfast). It's just kind of expected, not something you should have to request!

So, you can count me out if the only way I can get in is to have to share a plot with someone else - especially if I have to be on the bottom. On trains, and years ago at CYO camp, I always hated the bottom bunk, and, without having to drive this point into the ground any further, you can just give my slot to someone else if having to share a bunk-grave with someone else is the only way to get in. You can call me old fashioned if you want to, but I'd rather rot in the tub until I was mulch and then just be rinsed down the drain, than to rot two feet beneath somebody else's slowly decomposing carcass. But, if you can bend the rules in my regard, and give me a plot of my own with good drianage, I'm all yours.

Also, I'd like to know if there are any rules on the FONT SIZE on tombstones, and what the policy is on co-interning small pets.

Planning way ahead I hope,

Lazlo Toth

February 19, 1998

REPLY TO
ATTENTION OF

Public Affairs Office

Mr. Lazlo Toth
Post Office Box 245
Fairfax, California 94978

Dear Mr. Toth:

Thank you for your interest in Arlington National Cemetery.

Enclosed is a copy of the burial eligibility requirements at Arlington National Cemetery. Based on the information you provided us, you do not meet those requirements. I hope this information will be of help to you.

Space assignment in Arlington National Cemetery is assigned on an as-needed basis. No site can be reserved and only one gravesite will be assigned per family. If a spouse or eligible child dies first, space will be assigned provided the service member agrees in writing to be buried in the same site. Family members are buried with the veteran. Strangers do not share the same gravesite. Pets may not be interred at Arlington National Cemetery.

Rules and regulations governing headstones do exist. A fact sheet from the Veterans Affairs website is enclosed and will provide more information about headstones. Individuals may choose to erect private markers and monuments at their own expense in lieu of Government headstones. Private markers and headstones are only permitted in sections of the cemetery in which private markers were authorized as of January 1, 1947. Private markers and headstones will be approved only with the understanding that the purchaser will make provision for its future maintenance should repairs become necessary.

Again, thank you for your interest in Arlington National Cemetery.

Sincerely,

Charles D. Childers
Colonel, U.S. Army
Public Affairs Officer

February 25,1998

Director of Admissions
San Diego ZOO
San Diego, California

LAZLO TOTH
P.O. BOX 245
FAIRFAX, CA. 94978-0245

Dear Diretor,

I am writing to inquire if you allow animals at the zoo.

I would like to bring my dogs.

I have pointed out wild animals to them on television, and it always seems to perk their interest.

Now I would like them to be able to witness these beasts first hand, instead of having to be caged up in the car while I go in alone.

Lazlo Toth

Lazlo Toth

The Zoological Society of San Diego

March 25, 1998

Lazlo Toth
P.O. Box 245
Fairfax, CA 94978-0245

Dear Mr. Toth:

Thank you for your letter regarding bringing your dogs to the San Diego Zoo. Unfortunately, we do not allow dogs or any other pets on Zoo grounds. The only exception to this rule is registered service animals who assist the physically challenged.

Although it may seem like an enriching experience for your dogs to see wild animals first paw, it may create undue stress on your dogs as well as the animals that make up our Zoo. Even service animals are only allowed in certain areas of the Zoo for only a limited amount of time. We have found that members of our primate collection as well as many other species become extremely uneasy in the presence of a dog.

If you need a place for your dogs to stay during your visit to the San Diego Zoo, the following is a listing of local kennels:

Animal Center of San Diego	(619)299-7387
Fon Jon Kennels	(619)273-2266
Mission Valley Kennel	(619)282-0022
Morena Pet Hospital	(619)275-0888

Thank you for your understanding regarding our policy. We look forward to your visit to the World-Famous San Diego Zoo!

Sincerely,

Lori A. O'Connor
Operations Department
San Diego Zoo

Post Office Box 551, San Diego, California 92112-0551 USA Telephone (619) 231-1515 FAX (619) 231-0249

*Accredited by the American Zoo and Aquarium Association
and American Association of Museums*

LAZLO TOTH
P.O. BOX 245
FAIRFAX, CA. 94978-0245

August 21, 1998

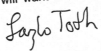

President William Jefferson Clinton
The White House
Washington, D.C.

Dear Mister President,

If you would have just delivered your "It Was Wrong" speech with the same passion and conviction as your "I did not have Sex with That Woman - Miss Lewinski" speech, all your problems might have been history by now.

But I read that you were told by some of your advisors (probably Gore), that if you apologized more sincerely, it may have made you appear weak on the brink of your vacation and your sneak missile attack on the janitor and his family at the pharmaceutical factory in Sudan.

So, instead of just coming off looking like a dog who just won't stay on the porch, you deceided instead to attack the dog catcher.

<u>That</u> speech "was wrong", and "inappropriate" as well, and so you had to pay the piper, and have the nation watch you going off to Martha's Vinyard holding your dog's leash instead of your wife's hand, and looking to the world like a man who is thinking to himself, "Is the current condition of the world in a mid-life crisis, or is it me?". The answer is obvious - Both!

But!, it's also obvious that THAT WOMAN, Miss Monkeyshine, set you up. If she's old enough to get a job at the Whitehouse, she's old enough to behave herself there, instead of looming around the halls, showing off her new sweaters, and parading past your oval office like a fly circling a Wendy's wrapper.

<u>My advise to you now?</u>
Dig up the video tape of Vice President Gore doing the Macarena at the I996 Demo convention. Everybody looks stupid when they Macarena, but he has a look on his face like he's so <u>proud</u> he learned it, and wants to show everyone how well he does it - it's just pathetic!

When people see that, nobody will want to impeach you, everyone will <u>beg</u> you to stay!

Lazlo Toth

Lazlo TOTH
Box 245 Fairfax California 94978

Newt Gringrich (R-Georgia)
C/o United States House of Representatives
Washington, D.C.

Dear Newt,   **With a** *tear running down his right cheek, House Speaker Newt Gingrich bows his head in prayer Saturday during a weekly GOP radio address.*

You have resigned as majority leader of the U.S. Congress after the stunning defeat your party partook a few Tuesday's ago.

So, why did your Contract with America fail?
You promised to vote on ten items - "The Ten Commitments", and you delivered the meat.

Welfare reform? Balanced budget? Tax cut? Yes. Yes. Yes.

Did you reform the IRS? No, but you meant to. Was there medicare reform? yes. some. Anti drugs legeslation? Intelligence and Military Increases? YES YES YES, again and again and again, calmly and systamatically you kept a straight face and put the pork on the cookie sheet.

So, what went wrong? Why did your boat belly up?

Was it because you didn't have sex preformed on you by some intern with a hall pass who couldn't get a date except with a guy who couldn't leave his house?

Would people have liked you more if you were caught eating Oysters in bed with Cher and Congressperson Mary Bono?, or if there was surveillance camera video tape of you visiting a crack house on a week night?

No, you were accused of misjudging the ethical standards of the American people, but what I think you really misjudged was their attention span. By the time of the election, they were well over the shock of the scandal and had moved on to parroting back the line that they were "sick and tired of hearing about Monica Lewinski".

Who would ever think that IMPEACHMENT would be basically a case of TIMING, and that in the end, Clinton would still be IN, and it would be YOU who would be leavin' on the midnight train.

Once again, they blame the Captain, not the iceberg. Once again, the crowd cries out "Ba-rab-bas!".

JUSTICE! - it should be a four letter word!

Buon Newt!

Lazlo

Lazlo Toth

from the poetry pad of
Lazlo Toth
Member: American Federation of Independent Poets
==================
November. 15, 1998

Senator John Glenn
U.S. Senate
Washington, D.C.

Mr. Lazlo Toth
P.O. Box 245
Fairfax, CA 94978

Dear Senator Glenn,

    I Sit, Write,
Talk   Dream
B O U N D

D O W N

like MOSS
on a
R O C K

G R A V I T Y .

Not you
P A T R I O T
Spaceman
W A R M
C O L D
WAR
H E R O
youdidit
4.
GOD
COUNTRY
GRAVITY
and
GERIATRIX
W e l C O M E
B A C K
AGAIN
JOHN GLENN !

Welcome back to Earth, the best Planet
of all the planets we know of so far,

Lazlo Toth

Lazlo Toth

JOHN GLENN
OHIO

United States Senate

WASHINGTON, DC 20510-3501

December 18, 1998

COMMITTEES:

- GOVERNMENTAL AFFAIRS
- ARMED SERVICES
- SELECT COMMITTEE ON INTELLIGENCE
- SPECIAL COMMITTEE ON AGING

Mr. Lazlo Toth
P. O. Box 245
Fairfax, California 94978

Dear Mr. Toth:

Thank you for contacting me regarding my flight on the space shuttle Discovery. I am sorry that I cannot give you a more personal reply, but I have been flooded with mail recently and I want to try to see to it that everyone gets a response.

I am happy to report that the nine day flight was a success and exceeded all my expectations. We had a busy mission, with 83 experiments on board and deployment of the Spartan satellite as our major tasks. My primary experiments involved the study of sleeplessness and muscle changes in an older person. The experiments went smoothly and while it is too early to determine their results, I am hopeful that the information learned will encourage further aging research in space and one day lead to new treatments for illnesses that afflict the elderly.

I was fortunate to be working with a fine group of astronauts - individuals as dedicated and capable as those I worked with when I entered the space program almost 40 years ago. Space exploration requires close teamwork that now transcends age, gender and nationality. I am pleased to say that this was evident among our crew and worked well.

Seeing earth again in all its fragile beauty and vivid color was a particular highlight and one that is hard to adequately describe. I was reminded again of how there are no country boundaries when viewed from space and how all humanity share a common interest in protecting this beautiful planet we call earth.

With the coming International Space Station, the next-generation space shuttle and Hubble telescope, follow-on probes to Mars and many other worthy projects, the future of our space program is bright. I think we should aim even higher for the 21st century and urge the President and Congress to increase our investment in the space program so that we can go to places that currently only exist in the imagination.

Thank you again for your interest in my flight and our space program.

Best regards.

Sincerely,

John Glenn

John Glenn
United States Senator

JG:sok

Christmas 1998

Mr. Lazlo Toth
P.O. Box 245
Fairfax, CA 94978-0245

Her Royalness Queen Elizabeth Windsor
Head of England
Buckingham Palace
London, England

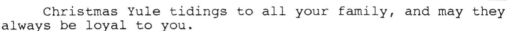

Dear Royal Queen Highness,

Christmas Yule tidings to all your family, and may they always be loyal to you.

I saw this article in the newspaper and thought you'd like to have it to show around the palace.

A similar thing happened to me once.

It was late at night, and it was raining, and out of nowhere! this deer is running across the road. I slam on the brakes just in time, but! <u>another</u> deer, who must have been running right behind the other deer, slams into the side of my car.

My passenger side door was all dented in, and then, my insurance company wouldn't pay. They say I'm covered if I hit a deer, but not if a deer hits me. They say "the insurance of the party that hit <u>you</u> should pay". I tell them, the party that ran into me does not have insurance, the party has HOOFS!

That deer, just like your pheasant, was still breathing.
I could tell by looking at his nostrils. So, to help him out, just like you did, I tried to speed up his dispatch, so I could get him out of the road.

Queen Highness, I was just wringing his neck for about TWO SECONDS, when UP!, THUMP!, he's on his feet, and bolting down the road. We go down through somebody's back yard, then we're back out on the road again, then we're back in more back yards, till finally he throws me off. I hurt my leg, and I didn't even know where I was. And I couldn't call 911 for help because I couldn't remember the number. That's how confused I was. I knew it started with a nine, but I couldn't remember what number came next. But it didn't matter, because nobody would let me in their house to use their phone because they all said I was too wet. Finally, somebody called me a cab. And the cab took forever to get there.

We are Mountains and an Ocean and Iceberg's apart, but we have both experienced similar animal—related events. Thank you.

Your cousin,
Lazlo Toth

Lazlo

Catholics for Jesus

==================

 Mr. Lazlo Toth
P.O. Box 245
Fairfax, CA 94978

Lazlo Toth
co-chair

Pope John Paul II
Vatican City
Vatican (State)

1 - 1 - 1 9 9 9
M C M X C I X

Dear Your Holiness,

First of all I want to say Happy New Year 1999, or, in Latin, Felix Annus Novum - MCMXCIX.

It's hard to believe that the GRANDUS MILLINIMUS ARRRIVUM SO SOONUM.

It's amazing to me how much Latin sounds like how Indians talk in cowboy movies. Maybe they came over here years go on some former land bridge that used to connect America with Rome. That's what I was thinking, but that's not why I'm writing now.

Holiness, there's only one year to go, and I don't know about you, but I feel the new millinium is coming towards us from behind.

Like a sneak attack we were warned was coming, but not from the direction we expected.

But, yes, it's right around the blocK, just waiting for us - like a giant water balloon.

Holiness, celestial events pull me to write to you now because recently astronomers announced that next month the Full Moon is going to be 3 times brighter than a normal full moon. They say at night, not only will your shadow appear way bigger, but that your shadow will even have it's own shadow.

They say the moon will be so close to Earth, that the tides will go both ways at once, and that if fish had bigger brains and were able to think as well as we do, they would be totally confused.

Then, last night, I had a dream where I saw a cloud encrusted woman, who looked a lot like our LADY OF FATIMA, standing in front of a large group of people, and she asked the crowd, <u>"Tell me, is it still now?"</u>, and they answered back, in unison, <u>"YES Not Yet"</u>.

So, what do you think that means? I am hoping you could put some light on the matter.

Lazlo Toth

---------- -----------

Toth Upholstery
Seat Covers for Miniture Cars our Specialty
Compare our prices!

Protects your minitures
from Sun and Dust

NEW!
We Make Miniture Futons
for Dolls Houses
compare our prices

FREE MINITURE CAR COVER
WITH EVERY TWO MINITURE
CARS REUPHOLSTERED

January 14, 1999

MARK THOMPSON
Anchor Man / Host
GUINESS BOOK OF WORLD RECORDS SHOW
Box 4361
Hollywood, California

Dear Mr. Thompson,

I tuned in too late and missed your story about the guy who could squirt milk out of his eyes, but your story about <u>The Longest Living Male Siamese Twins</u> was inspiring, especially the part about what they do when one wants to go to bed and the other one wants to stay up and watch television. (They do whatever the bigger one wants.).

Mr. Thompson, at this time I would like to report a possible World Record for:
<u>The Longest Living Male To Go Without Sleep</u>.

I loaned money to my former brother-in-law, who wrote me that he would not sleep until he had paid me back.
That was <u>twenty</u> one years ago.

Would you please let me know, - <u>What is the longest a person has gone without sleep?</u>

Could this possibly be a new world record?

Lazlo Toth

Lazlo Toth

July 19, 1999

Lazlo Toth
P.O. Box 245
Fairfax, CA 94978

Dear Lazlo,

Thank you for your comments regarding "Guinness World Records: *Primetime*" and for your suggestions on possible record-breaking ideas. We receive an overwhelming number of suggestions, and unfortunately, we cannot consider your idea for the show at this time.

We recommend you contact Guinness Media, publisher of the "Guinness Book of Records." Their contact information is as follows:

Kim Stram
c/o Guinness Media
6 Landmark Square
Stamford, Conn. 06901-2704
203/967-7910 (fax)
infousa@guinnessrecords.com

We appreciate your taking the time to contact us and hope you keep watching "Guinness World Records: *Primetime*" on our new day and time, Tuesdays at 8 PM ET/PT on FOX, starting June 22.

As you can imagine, we receive an overwhelming amount of mail from our viewers, so we apologize if this response has been slow in getting to you and appreciate your patience.

"Guinness Primetime" Staff

P.O. Box 4361, Hollywood, CA 90028 • www.lmnotv.com

Produced in association with Guinness Publishing Limited

Lazlo Toth
P.O. Box 245
Fairfax, California
USA 94978

June 20, 1999

Vice President Albert Gore
c/o The White HOuse
Washington, D.C.

Dear Vice President Gore,

     You are under fire again. They say your camapign is
stalled, they even recruited your wife to give your camapign
"a human touch". At least they got off your back for saying
you invented the internet.

     Actually, what you said was, "I took the initiative in
creating the internet". Again, they misinterpeted your
intentions. You just wanted to get credit for being a <u>part</u>
of the start of the internet, not the whole thing, what's
the matter with them!

     I had an uncle who took the initiative of putting a
cherry on top of half of a grapefruit. I understand that
before he came up with the cheery idea, they used to use
little pieces of banana on the top of grapefruit, but after
he instituted the cherry initiative, everyone said, "How is
it someone didn't come up with this idea before?", it's
wonderful!, "You're a true grapefruit genius!".

     But then, one of his fellow Knights (of Columbus),
spread rumors that it wasn't true, that my Uncle didn't
invent the idea of putting the cherry on top, that it had
been done before somewhere elce. They started saying he had
"illusions of grapefruit grandeur".

     All I kbnow is after he was accused, he never set a foot
in the lodge again, not even to go to the fish fry's.
     That's the reason, too, of how he got burnt, becuase he
was frying his own fish, at home. It wouldn't have happened
if only he had said, "Yes, perhaps someone elce may have done
it before him, but to the best of his knowledge he didn't
know it at the time, but!, even if he did, he didn't mean it
to be taken that it was solely His initiative, that he wwas
just PART of the idea".

     Mister Vice President, I feel your
pain, good luck in the campaign,

                    Lazlo Toth
                    Lazlo Toth

July 23, 1999

Mr. Lazlo Toth
Post Office Box 245
Fairfax, California   94978

Dear Mr. Toth,

Thank you for writing and sharing your thoughts and views with me. I appreciate hearing from you.

As we move toward the turn of the century, we face many challenges. For the past six years, I have been working hard to get the country back on the right track. Hearing from citizens like you is tremendously helpful. It is essential to recognize and respond to the needs and demands of all Americans.

I am determined to continue to focus our efforts on our most critical needs – creating better opportunities and economic security for working Americans, maintaining our nation's security, protecting the environment, and establishing a more efficient government.

At the same time, Tipper and I also contribute to issues that do not receive day-to-day national attention. Every year since 1993 we have both run in the "Race for the Cure," an activity to raise awareness and funds in the fight against breast cancer. In addition, Tipper has worked countless hours for the benefit of children and for those suffering from mental illness. While we are pleased with the progress we have made on many fronts, we know we still have miles to go. We are both committed to an America where no one is left behind.

I am grateful to receive your letter, and value your insights. I will carefully consider your comments as we work to meet the challenges of the next century.

For further information about the campaign, I hope you will visit the campaign's website at www.algore2000.com.

Again, thank you for writing and for your interest in a better future for our nation.

Sincerely,

Al Gore

Washington, D.C. Headquarters:
Gore 2000
P.O. Box 18237
Washington, D.C. 20036
www.algore2000.com

Tennessee Headquarters:
Gore 2000
P.O. Box 24387
Nashville, TN 37202
www.algore2000.com

Paid for by Gore 2000, Inc.
Contributions to Gore 2000, Inc. are not tax deductible for federal income tax purposes.

COMMITTEE ON CORRESPONDENCE

P.O. Box 245. Fairfax, California. 94978 USA

FOUNDERS

Samuel Adams

Joseph Warrens

BIRTHDAY COMMITTEE

Lazlo Toth

Five milestones, but Prince William skips to study for exams

June 21, 2000

Queen Elizabeth Windsor (Head)
Queen of England
Buckingham Palace
London England

Dear Queen Elizabeth,

As head of the Windsors, I call on you to pass on my Happy Birthday to You greetings to each of everyone of your royal family members who are gathering today to celebrate all together (almost) the combined "birthdays of significance" that happen this jubilee new millennium summer — the time that will be known throughout the future as "The Summer of Birthdays of Significance" of the insignificant (so far) year 2000.

I know it's a "private party" (no commoners, except Lady Fergie, allowed), but I only wish I could be a fly on the royal wallpaper at your family's combined birthday celebration. It's amazing — all these "birthdays of significance" on the same summer, it baggles my mind:

The <u>Queen Mother</u>- age 100 in August, knock on wood.
 Your Sister - <u>Princess Anne</u>, 5
Your Son — <u>Prince Andrew</u>, chronologically, age 40
 You Daughter — <u>Princess Margaret</u> — 70 (490)
And your grandson, <u>Prince William</u>, 18 — who bailed.

Highness, I put my calculator and math knowledge to work, and as far as my current numbers add up, all together the summer birthday years in your family add up to a total of 228 years, or, in dog years — 1588 years.

So, from across the pond, and over the fence, HAPPY BIRTHDAY of Significance! from all of us who couldn't be there .

So, cut the Cakes! Serve the Tea!
Let bygones be bygones!,

Your cousin,

Lazlo Toth

Lazlo Toth

Mega-Birthday Bash for British Royal Family

BUCKINGHAM PALACE

29th June, 2000

Dear Mr Toth,

I am commanded by The Queen to thank you for your letter and for sending your message of good wishes on the occasion of the birthdays of Queen Elizabeth The Queen Mother, Prince William, The Duke of York, The Princess Royal and The Princess Margaret.

Your kind words are much appreciated and I am to thank you again for writing to Her Majesty at this time.

Yours sincerely

Mary Fanick

Lady-in-Waiting

Mr L. Toth

Mr. Lazlo Toth
P.O. Box 245
Fairfax, CA 94978-0245

------------------   June 22, 2000

Delta Partners
Manager — Frequent Claims Department
Service Center Central
Atlanta, Ga. 30320

Dear Plan Manager:

    I have not heard from my Dentist in over two weeks.
His assistant say's he doesn't return calls unless people are
in pain, but she wouldn't believe me, so that is why I am
writing directly to you personally to ask if you found out
yet from the Lab about when my <u>CROWN</u> is coming in.

    Before he started refusing to talk to me again, he said
it was up to you (DELTA) how much you would pay for the
CROWN, and he said he thought Crowns for a dental plan like
mine are made in Korea, and that it could take months.

    I want you to know I'm not the type to put the blame on
the Dental Plan, or the store where I bought the Candy Corn.
The cost rests on your shoulders, but the blame rests on
mine. I knew the candy probably was left over from Holloween,
that it probably wouldn't taste real Fresh, and that was
probably the reason it was priced so inexpensively, but I
never thought it would taste so hard. It was like biting
into a curb.

    Also, he said if the temporary crown bends again, that my
insurance plan probably wouldn't cover it next time.

    <u>Question:</u> How many bent temporary crowns is a person
allowed for under a plan like mine, and do I have to pay for
all of it or just a percentage if it happens more than twice?

Thank-you.

Lazlo Toth

▲.Delta

Delta Air Lines, Inc.
Post Office Box 20980
Atlanta, Georgia 30320-2980

404 715 1450
www.delta-air.com

August 24, 2000

Mr. Lazlo Toth
P. O. Box 245
Fairfax, California 94978

Dear Mr. Toth:

Your recent letter was forwarded to our office for handling. We generally respond to passengers who have problems with their travel such as delayed flights, luggage or ticketing problems.

Unfortunately, your letter has left us somewhat baffled. If your dental problems are related to travel with us, we will be happy to review further but will require additional information from you. We will need the flight numbers, date of travel and a brief description of the incident.

We treat any report of customer dissatisfaction very serious and would like to review this matter on your behalf. As soon as we receive the requested information, we will respond accordingly.

Sincerely,

Glenda J. Lock

Glenda J. Lock
Manager
Customer Care

GLL:lgx

LAZLO TOTH

Mr. Lazlo Toth
P.O. Box 245
Fairfax, CA 94978-0245

7.
7.
2000.

Consumers Services
Kimberly Clark Corporation
Dept.KEFT-85 / Kleenex Tissue Division
P.O. Box 2020
Neenah, WI 54957

Dear Kleenex Division Leader,

I purchase your attractively decorated square boxes of
KLEENEX whenever I'm having company over. I find that besides
adding a touch of class to my bathroom, it also serves as a
convenient back up for when I run out of toilet paper.

One P r o b l e m :
It's impossible to get the first few pieces of Kleenex out
of the box in one piece. The Kleenex are packed so tight in
there, you can't get them out without tearing them.

To overcome this D E F E C T :
I suggest you make the box bigger. By simply enlarging
the box by "One-quarter of an Inch", this problem can be
solved once and for all.

Lazlo Toth

P.S.
For wedding gifts, I have found that when
the boxes are empty, they can be filled with
sand and made into book ends.

Kimberly-Clark

July 28, 2000

Mr. Lazlo Toth
PO Box 245
Fairfax, CA 94978-0245

Dear Mr. Toth:

Thank you for contacting us about KLEENEX® EXPRESSIONS® facial tissue. We appreciate the opportunity to respond.

We are sorry that you received packages that did not dispense properly and can understand your frustration when the tissue tears as you remove it from the carton. This is sometimes due to humid storage conditions which cause the tissue to "swell" from the absorption of moisture. Whether or not humidity was the cause of tearing, please accept our apology for the inconvenience. Your comments will be forwarded to those involved with this product.

We would be very pleased if you would consider using our product again, at no cost to you, by redeeming the enclosed coupons. Thank you again for contacting us and for giving us an opportunity to make amends.

Sincerely,

Patti Fercy

Patti M. Fercy
Consumer Specialist

PMF/LJS

5228736A

89

=TOTHWORKS=
LIGHTS =CAMERA= BIRDS
POB245FAIRFAX94978

=   =   =

From The Desk Of
LAZLO TOTH

7-21-00

Governor George W. Bush III
Governor's Mansion
Austin, Texas

Dear Future President Governor Bush,

You were very impressive last night on Larry King CNN Show.

I think even Larry was won over when you talked about GUN CONTROL, and how, under your leadership, the State of Texas is giving out FREE TRIGGER LOCKS to anyone who owns a hand gun.
Governor, HOMERUN!

I am enclosing four 33 cent stamps to pay for First Class postage for ONE TRIGGER LOCK.
I'm pretty sure that will be enough to cover the cost, unless it's heavier than I expect, but if it is I'd appreciate it if you would still send it First Class, instead of by slower mail, and then I'll pay the postage due when it arrives.

I don't expect the taxpayers of TEXAS, or your campaign committee, to foot the bill for the postage, too - the FREE safety lock is generous enough, but thanks anyway.
And, don't worry about me, I'll be fine. There's just been a lot of pressure here lately on the Lot, and once I get my free Trigger Lock I'm sure I'll be getting back to feeling more normal.

Good luck in the campaign. I feel that In this election, the candidate who the people think is lying less than the other one, is going to win. You're in the lead so far.

Lazlo Toth

Lazlo Toth

The Knights of Serra
BLESSED JUNIPERO SERRA SAINTHOOD NOW

Lazlo Toth
Knight /Auction Director

BoP 245. 94978
Fairfax Headquarters
BAJA ALBERTA DIVISION

August 4, 2000

Queen Mother Windsor-Head
Buckingham Palace
London, England

Dear Your Royal Highness Queen Mom,

Happy 100th Birthday to You. You make everybody feel young, thank you.

I got a nice letter back from your granddaughter. She mentioned that she was in waiting, but you couldn't tell it from the photos I saw of her (People Magazine) that were taken at the big shin-dig. She must only be about four months gone, am I right?

And it said, "Prince William was the only Royal missing".

Correct me if I'm wrong, but I noticed that the Duke of Earl was also not in any of the photographs as well. I would think he would have come even if he wasn't invited – as we know, nothing can stop him.

I have to say this – of all the people at the party YOU looked like you were having the most "merry 'ol time" of everybody. I'll bet there's one title nobody ever gave you - "Designated Driver", am I right? I learned a long time ago that Gin is not a summer time drink. Have you ever tried Absinthe? That's what Toulouse-Lautrec used to drink, you probaly knew him, that's why I mention it. Over here, I think to get it, you have a precription.

QUESTION: I saw a picture of you recently and you were only wearing ONE GLOVE. I thought, "No, look!, she lost her glove!".

But, in another magazine, you were wearing just ONE GLOVE again.

Queen Mom, if it's not betraying some top secret masonic code, or something, could you tell me WHY you just wear just ONE GLOVE a lot of the time? What does it mean?

And, if you only just use one glove all the time on purpose, - do you think you might consider sending the other one to my prayer group for us to auction off at our fund raiser on October 19th?, to help raise money to support our effort to canonize Fr. Junipero Serra, for Patron Saint of Lupus and Scoliosis (curvature of the spine). So far, Marie Osmond sent us a scarf, and we'd love to have a glove from you, but if you'd rather send something else, that would be fine, too.

Many thanks, many more birthdays,

Lazlo Toth

UNWAVERING

Lazlo Toth
CALIFORNIA

By Jeff Mitchell, Reuters

On the trail: George W. Bush
with Dick Cheney in Casper.

August 16, 2000

Mr. Dick Cheney
CEO in Transition
Halliburton Company
500 N. Akard
Dallas, TEXAS

Dear Dick,

When Geo. W. Bush picked you to help him pick the person
to become his running mate, he picked the right man because
the man that that man picked was you.

Yes!, YOU! — the Man who picked himself, the man who made
the perfect choice of himself, and all America is happy that
you did.   Stand up! You deserve it!

I'll always be grateful for that Memo you sent me back
in 1991,   when I was first being considered for the DESERT
SHIELD/DESERT STORM medal, for my efforts to reestablish
captive animals in Kuwait.

Even though, in the end, I was found to be partially
ineligible mainly just because I didn't face the same exact
hazards as military personnel (bombs, bullets, vaccinations),
we both know I did my best.

And, although, I know, and you know, too, that I wish
I had received the medal, I'll never forget the fact that you
returned the money.

I'm going to say it one more time, forgive me, but I
mean it - Dick Cheney, you made a good choice, Dick Cheney!
You picked the right man!

Let's get together for dinner when I'm in town, I'd like to
do that.

Next Stop - Washington, D.C.!
You can do it, you've just got to!

Lazlo Toth

Vice President Albert W. Gore
C/o President Bill Clinton
The White House
Washington, D.C.

Mr. Lazlo Toth
P.O. Box 245
Fairfax, CA 94978-0245

August 17, 2000

Dear Vice President Gore,

    I just got finished watching television, and you were on just about all the channels.

    Instead of saying, "I stand here tonight as my own man", I think it would have been better if you said, "I'm HERE tonight as my own man".
    You didn't have to say, "I <u>STAND</u> here tonight", they can see you standing there.

    Also, I wonder why you didn't mention, NOT ONE WORD, about Elian Gonzalas. Now that he's back with Fidel, I guess he's history's newspaper, is that what you're telling me?

    Other than those two points, and the delivery, you did fine.
Form and Function, separate suites, am I right?

I'm my own man, too,

Lazlo Toth

Lazlo Toth

Enclosed: $3 CASH:
 One for "GORE 2000" button.
 One for "More Gore 2004" —or, "Liberman" button.
 One for "Hilary for Senator" button.
 No bumper stickers. Thank you.

TTTTT TTTTT oo ooooo oo o oooo TT TTTTT T H HH HH H

.p.o. box 2 4 5. Fairfax California. 94 978.

September 6, 2000

Glenda J. Lock
Manager- Customer Care (Dental)
Delta Airlines Inc.
P.o. Box 20980
Atlanta, Georgia 30320

Dear Customer Care Manager,
 I am not dissatisfied. I didn't say I was dissatisfied.
I just asked when my Crown was coming in.
 Here is the "additional Information" you requested:
 I did not break my tooth while flying on your airplane, my Dental
problems are not related to travel with you, it happened in my car,
while driving, coming home from the store.
 And a Brief description of the Incident:
 1. June 8, 2000- 1 pm - I purchase small package of CANDY CORN (out
of season), at LONG'S DRUG STORE in REDHILL.
 2. 1:10 pm. - I attempt to chew (bite down) on candy corn.
  Tooth (#38) BREAKS.
 3. 1: 11 pm – Sharp PAIN coming from region where tooth #38 was.
 4. 1:13 pm. Instead of continuing driving home, I turn in the direction of
  my Dentist's Office.
 5. 1:22 pm. - Arrive at Dentist office, short wait, ICE.
 6. 2:15 pm – Dentist installs "Temporary" crown. I'm told I have to wait
  for authorization for payment from the DELTA DENTAL Plan, and for
  the Permanent CROWN to arrive (from Korea).
 7. June 22, 2000 - I write to you asking when the crown is coming in.
 8. July, 2000 - My Dentist is in Chile visiting relatives.
 9. August 24,2000 – you write back to me for additional information
  and my Flight Number. I don't remember the last time I flew on your
  airline, but I remember that your In-Flight Magazine was very nice.
  If it was made with thinner paper, it would make the airplane lighter,
  and inable passengers to carry-on more of their own belongings.
  Also, the Bathrooms: TOO SMALL!, you can hardly wash in there.
 10. Now.

 I think perhaps we can can expidite things if you could tell me exactly
where in Korea the Crown is coming in from. It would help me to grasp
the timetable. I heard that there is a big famine going on in NORTH
Korea, so if it's coming from there, it could be the factory is working at
half staff because of the nutricianal inadequatcies. Maybe that's the hold
up. I'm baffled, too. If you've received any additional information about
approximately WHEN it's due in, I'd appreciate knowing.
 Thank you.

Lazlo Toth
Lazlo Toth

Delta Air Lines, Inc.
Post Office Box 20980
Atlanta, Georgia 30320-2980

404 715 1450
www.delta-air.com

October 2, 2000

Mr. Lazlo Toth
P. O. Box 245
Fairfax, California 94978

Dear Mr. Toth:

Thank you for your prompt response to my request for additional information. Please accept my sincere apology, I regret any misunderstanding.

Unfortunately, we cannot provide you with the information requested. If you are a Delta employee, our Human Resources department will be happy to assist you but I believe your dentist can best provide you with this information.

Thank you again for writing.

Sincerely,

Glenda J. Lock
Manager
Customer Care

GLL:lgx

TO: Governor George W. Bush
BUSH FOR PRESIDENT
Austin, Texas

FROM: Lazlo Toth
P.O. Box 245
Fairfax 94978 Calif.

Re: The First Debate. October 3, 2000. Boston.

The press said, " BUSH, GORE come out EVEN ", but I say – T.I.E.
As I watched, I kept score by putting down PLUS or MINUS for everything from Neckware to Unnatural Facial Gestures, to how well each of you answered the Questions.
At the end, my grand total tally was - MINUS 90 for Gore, and – MINUS 90 for you, - a dead even TIE!

Gore said, "I was morally against the Vietnam War, but I went because I knew that if I didn't go, someone else from my hometown would have to go".
I gave him minus ten for that, and minus ten for you for not pointing out that if GORE refused to go and someone else from his hometown was drafted in his place, then that person could have refused to go, too.
Question: What if they gave a war and nobody went except Albert Gore?
Answer: The war would have been over a lot sooner.
After you said that you sent your kids to Public Schools, and he chirped in and said he sent his kids to Public Schools, too, I'm surprised he didn't say that he sends his kids to public school because if he didn't, somebody elces kids would have to go.

Governor, W., please send me a "BUSH for President" button as soon as possible. Voting day is creeping near, and, as President Nixon used to say, "One hand washes the other one". All I want is a button, that's all I'm asking for.

Help me help you ,

Lazlo Toth

There is no need to pay
for buttons! Thanks for
your support!
        Bush/Cheney 2000

LAZLO TOTH
California
REGISTERED

TO: Vice President ALBERT W. GORE
    GORE FOR PRESIDENT Headquarters
    Nashville, Tennessee

FROM: Lazlo Toth

Re: The Second Debate.   October 11, 2000

     In the second debate, they say Bush was trying hard not to smirk, and you were trying not to act like a jerk.   Bush wanted to come off as less cocky, and you wanted to come off as less corny.

     Bottom line - the race is <u>neck and neck</u>.

     But!, who ever it was who advised you to <u>stop</u> throwing the audience kisses, and to <u>stop</u> always touching your heart when they clapped, should be Knighted!.
    A lot of people who disliked seeing you do that at the first debate, dislike you less now. I wouldn't say that puts you on the COMEBACK trail, but you're off the respirator.

     But the best thing you did? SWITCHING TIES!
  And, <u>Powder Blue</u> was the perfect choice. I could see that Bush seemed really thrown off guard when he saw it. He must have been expecting you to be wearing a RED tie again, and WHAMMO! you could see he was stunned.

     It was a curveball <u>nobody</u> expected. Blue! Now! I think you've rerounded the bend!

     I bet a lot of people wondered if you just came up with that yourself, or if it was planned way in advance by your consultants. One things for sure, it worked!

     But, what's next? Who should you be?

     My advise for how you should act for the remaining three weeks of the campaign? I think you should try to act like - <u>Robert DeNiro</u>.

     I think you can pull it off - you two are about the same height. It's not going to be easy, BUT! if BUSH keeps going up in the polls, it's worth a shot.

Lazlo Toth
P.O. Box 245
Fairfax, CA 94978-0245

Al Gore

President &
First Lady

► Vice President &
Mrs. Gore

Record of
Progress

The Briefing
Room

Gateway to
Government

Contacting the
White House

White House
for Kids

White House
History

White House
Tours

Vice Presid

Biography

Speeches

Initiatives

News Relea

Email the V

Virtual Libr

Welcome to my web page! You will find links to a wide range of information about my work as Vice President, the accomplishments and agenda of the Clinton-Gore Administration and programs and policies that affect you, your community and this nation.

Over the past eight years, we have been working hard to turn this country around. Moving from a time of recession, debt and doubt, we now enjoy an unprecedented era of prosperity, surplus and hope.

America is working again. Twenty-two million people have new jobs and economic security for their families.

The biggest budget deficits in history have been transformed into the biggest surpluses ever.

We are living in the longest period of economic growth ever experienced in our country.

Crime is down. Welfare rolls have been cut in half. And our federal government is smaller than it has been in 40 years.

The credit for these remarkable achievements belongs, first and foremost, to the American people. The Clinton-Gore Administration has always pursued policies that unlock the creativity, the ingenuity, and the hard work of the American people. That is why we will not rest until every American can fully participate in the remarkable economic success that so many have enjoyed in recent years.

I hope you'll browse this web page and learn more about the work we've done together and how we can go about making the changes Americans desire in order to secure a prosperous and peaceful future for our children.

Thank you once again for coming to my web site, and I hope you enjoy your visit!

Best wishes,

Unofficial Signature

La ZLO T O Th

11.
21.
2000.

Patti M. Fercy
Consumer Specialist
Kimberly Clarks Corporation
P.O. Box 220
Neenah, WI 54957

Dear Specialist Fercy.

Bad news. I'm still having trouble with your Kleenex.

I put one package of EXPRESSIONS in my refrigerator, as you suggested, and with the other coupon you sent for my research, I put one package in the trunk of my car.

PLUS, I purchased eight more with my own financing, for further testing, and stored those unopened packages of tissue in other places around my home (and garage).

Research:

I agree with you that the reason for the tissue "SWELL" is because of HUMIDITY, but after hours of experiments, spread out over a period of months with vast humidy differences, regardless of where I placed or stored the tissue, I was unable to get the first piece of Kleenex out of the carton without tearing it in two.

Research RESULTS:

Specialist Fercy, my research prooves that "swell" caused by humidy are not on the consumer's (STORAGE) end of the Kleenex chain, but that the humidy swell problem originates at your packaging plant, at packaging time, at the your factory, in Wisconsin.

Where to now? SOLUTION:

It seems cystal clear that your problem could be solved by moving you KLEENEX EXPRESSIONS packaging operations to a less humid zone of the country. My recommendation: Tucson.

But!, a far simpler solution, and much less expensive then relocating the entire operation to Arizona, would be to make the box bigger.

By simply enlarging the EXPRESSIONS package by "One-quarter of an inch", you can nip the whole swelling issue in the bud, and the plant stays in Wisconsin, and nobody has to move.

Lazlo Toth

⊛ Kimberly-Clark   Consumer Services

December 15, 2000

Mr. Lazlo Toth
PO Box 245
Fairfax, CA 94978-0245

Dear Mr. Toth:

Thank you for contacting Kimberly-Clark Corporation again.

It was thoughtful of you to give us your opinion about KLEENEX EXPRESSIONS tissue. Comments such as yours are very important in helping us know how consumers feel about our products. You can be sure we will share your comments with others involved.

Please accept the enclosed coupons because we value you as a customer. Thank you again for contacting us.

Sincerely,

Patti M. Fercy
Consumer Specialist

PMF/cl

5228736B

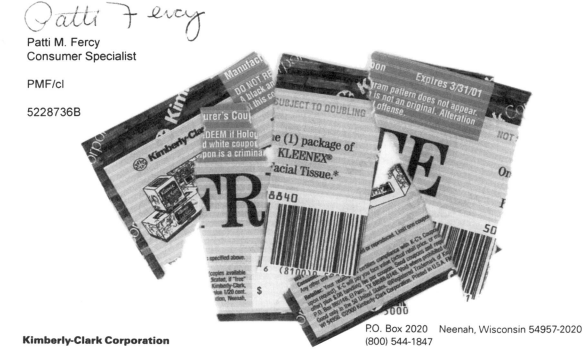

LAZLO TOTH
FREELANCE
FAIRFAXBOX24594978
STATE OF
CALIFORNIA

2. Kim Jong II asked for Albright's e-mail

. NOV. 1 1 . 0 0 .

Great Leader Kim Jong II
President Forever of North Korea (Peninsula)
Pyongyang, North Korea

Great Leader!,

TOOTH NUMBER	DATE OF SERVICE	CONTRACT CATEGORY	PROC. NO.	DESCRIPTION OF SERVICE	SL
30	04/17/00	CAST	02790	CAST HIGH NOBLE CROWN	
	04/17/00	DIAG			
	04/17/00	DIAG	Delta Dental Plan of California		

Great news! All the media over here is reporting the great success of your meetings with the Great Secretary of State great outgoing Madaline Albright.

Yes!, some say that wherever she goes, bombs follow. But I don't think you have to be concerned, the newspapers all said that you two really hit it off. They say they think she has a crush on you. That's why she got so excited when you asked her for her e-mail address. People say they hadn't seen her that happy since the fall of Slobodan Milosevic.

Great Leader, it was quite impressive to read that more than 100,000 of your workers acted out scenes of socialist glory by simulating, with shawls, the movement of the ocean.

I'm sure that impressed Madame Albright, but when I read about that, I just said to myself, with all those people out there waving around shawls, who! is minding the dental crown factories?

No wonder why my crown is delayed! My dental plan (Delta) will be baffled no more. Suddenly, - Mystery CLOSED! Case SOLVED!

FIVE DAYS! after our election, YES! we still don't know who's going to be President next, but! - the MAIL DOES NOT STOP!

I have enclosed the records provided to me by my Delta. If you could please forward it on to your leading underling in the province where my crown is being manufactured, I know that would help speed up the process.

Here's hoping that this breakthrough in relations between you and Madame (2 more months to go) Albright, will help open the door, if only briefly, towards more responsible shipping obligations.

Together!, let's strive to vow to move towards that goal,

Lazlo Toth

Please send me your picture
as soon as possible
so I can show it to my Dentist .

Mr. Hugh Hefner
Playboy Mansion
L.A., California

Mr. Lazlo Toth
P.O. Box 245
Fairfax, CA 94978-0245

Nov. 15, 2000

Dear Mr. Hefner,

It was pretty absurd when AL Gore, and the rest of the HAPPY FACES at the Democat convention FORBID Congressperson Sanchez from having a fund raiser at your mansion. These guys take money from Chinese bag men and Monks with no names, but thay reject your support because your image is beneath them? What a joke. To tar and feather these guys would be a waste of feathers. And tar.

I submit an idea for your magazine.
It is not about the evil, sex filled world of magazine publishing, no!, it is about the evil, sex filled world of politics.

The Title   <u>SPERM WARFARE</u>
    OR -   <u>The President's Condom Is Missing.</u>

In my story, U.S. President Dick Littlerock has sex in the Harding bedroom of the Whitehouse, with an attractive airline stewardess he thinks he may have met before.
But! it turns out she is really an Iraqi secret agent, sent to D.C. with the intent of tucking the President's used condom into a climate controled "pantie pocket", disguised as a label, in her underware.
Within hours, Littlerock's sperm is in a THERMOS, packed in DRY ICE (I'm still doing research on the technical terms), on a private jet to Bagdad. And in less than eight hours after the President asked her, "Aren't you going to stay to catch Tom Hanks on Letterman?", the "stewerdess" is in Iraq, passing the thermos, with the seed of the most powerful man in the world, over to Saddam Hussein's secret police, who rush it via armord car to an underground secret genetic lab - bunker, where 1000 fertile female volunteers wait to be impregnated. (NOTE: one dose load of male ejaculation contains over 300,000 sperm, so Saddam could make more than 1,000 " Baby Dick's" if he wanted to, and had sufficient refrigeration capabilities).
<u>Nine months later:</u>
Saddam uses these "Little Littlerocks", <u>as Genetic Shields</u>, to create a Baby-Hostage line of defence, to safeguard Iraq from attacks by the United States, <u>and</u> to obtain foreign revenue by demanding child support payments from President Littlerock. Littlerock denies ever meeting "That Stewerdess", and say's, "I didn't even hear her leave". After viewing photos of the babies he say's, "Most of them look more like George Stepanoplis than they do me". Stepanapolis say's he never met her either, but to him, "All babies look like Pat Buchanon".

Mr. Hefner!, What would a story like this pay if I could make it as long as I possibly could?

Lazlo Toth
Lazlo Toth

LAZLO TOTH
CaLIfOrnIA
November 18, 2000

Mr. Lazlo Toth
P.O. Box 245
Fairfax, CA 94978-0245

> *"You mean to tell me, Mr. Vice President, you're retracting your concession?"*
>
> **George W. Bush**
> on election night
>
> •
>
> *"You don't have to be snippy about it."*
>
> **Vice President Al Gore**

Vice President Al GORE
President Elect in Waiting
Gore 2000-01 Campaign Headquarters
P.O. Box 18237
Washington.d.c. 20036

Dear Vice President Gore,

One week and four days ago, the American people went to the polls to elect a new President. And eleven days later, it's <u>still</u> NECK and NECK.
It just doesn't stop.

That was a billiant move you made when you phoned Governor Bush to congradulate him on winning, and then calling him back a few minutes later and saying you changed your mind.
Why? Because it led to you saying your all time great quote of all time – "<u>You don't have to be snippy about it</u>".
If you had only used that line during the debates, you would have nailed down the Librarians vote, which would have given you the edge to win the election outright.
I looked in the famous book, THESAURUS Of QUOTATIONS, it's the controlling authority on these matters, and the word "SNIPPY" has never before been used in a famous quote. Congadulations! Another FIRST!

<u>ALert! Reminder</u>: It was one year ago you mentioned on the Don Imus show that Otkir Sultonov, you know, the Hallmark of Uzbekistan, had to remind you that Hamed Karoui's birthday was coming up, and you better get a card off to Tunisia <u>quick</u>.
What with all the hoppla these past eleven days, I was thinking you probably forgot again this year for sure, so I made a nice card and signed both our names. I just hope I spelled his name right.

I am sending a contribution to help pay towards the expenses for all the extra lawyers you had to hire for your Florida recount effort.
Now don't get snippy, but I want you to know I am also contributing to Governor Bush's continuing campaign.
All I know is, in the end, one of you will WIN and the other one will become President.

Good Luck to us all,

Lazlo Toth

P.S. Did anybody ever tell you that when you and Senator Lieberman stand next to each other, the two of you look just like Batman and Robin?

ENCL: $2.

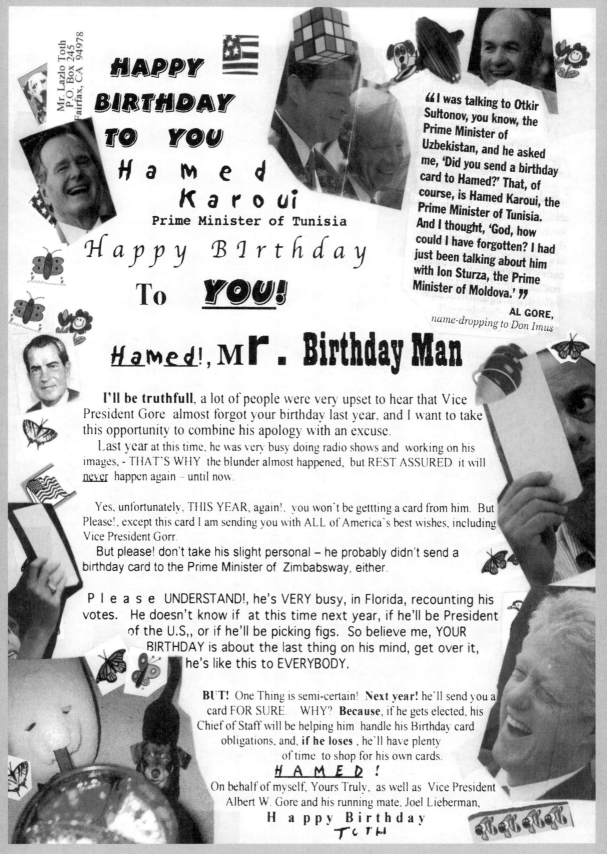

HAPPY BIRTHDAY TO YOU Hamed Karoui
Prime Minister of Tunisia

Happy BIrthday To *YOU!*

> "I was talking to Otkir Sultonov, you know, the Prime Minister of Uzbekistan, and he asked me, 'Did you send a birthday card to Hamed?' That, of course, is Hamed Karoui, the Prime Minister of Tunisia. And I thought, 'God, how could I have forgotten? I had just been talking about him with Ion Sturza, the Prime Minister of Moldova.'"
>
> — AL GORE,
> *name-dropping to Don Imus*

Hamed!, Mr. Birthday Man

I'll be truthfull, a lot of people were very upset to hear that Vice President Gore almost forgot your birthday last year, and I want to take this opportunity to combine his apology with an excuse.

Last year at this time, he was very busy doing radio shows and working on his images, - THAT'S WHY the blunder almost happened, but REST ASSURED it will <u>never</u> happen again – until now.

Yes, unfortunately, THIS YEAR, again!, you won't be gettting a card from him. But Please!, except this card I am sending you with ALL of America's best wishes, including Vice President Gorr.

But please! don't take his slight personal – he probably didn't send a birthday card to the Prime Minister of Zimbabsway, either.

P l e a s e UNDERSTAND!, he's VERY busy, in Florida, recounting his votes. He doesn't know if at this time next year, if he'll be President of the U.S,, or if he'll be picking figs. So believe me, YOUR BIRTHDAY is about the last thing on his mind, get over it, he's like this to EVERYBODY.

BUT! One Thing is semi-certain! **Next year!** he'll send you a card FOR SURE. WHY? **Because**, if he gets elected, his Chief of Staff will be helping him handle his Birthday card obligations, and, **if he loses**, he'll have plenty of time to shop for his own cards.

<u>H A M E D</u> !

On behalf of myself, Yours Truly, as well as Vice President Albert W. Gore and his running mate, Joel Lieberman,

H a p p y B i r t h d a y
Toth

TOTHWORKS
LIGHTS ACTION

P. O. BOX 245 FAIRFAX ...... CALIFORNIA 94978

Lazlo Toth
FOUNDER

Thursday 6 p.m.
November 23. 2000

16 DAYS SINCE ELECTION
DEADLOCK
DAY 16

Governor George W. Bush
President Elect in Waiting
Austin, T e x a s

Dear Governor,

Happy Thanksgiving. I just saw you on the tube, waving to the reporters who are all hanging around outside your ranchhouse gate, like dogs waiting to be thrown the turkey bone.

I tried something different for Thanksgiving this year – Salisbury Steak. I won't go into the details, but the bottom line is, next year, I'm back to eating Turkey.

Things have not been running smooth here at the Lot, my finances are a little too binding at the moment, and my prayers today are that at least they give me a little time before they try to put a lean on my property or my aurboritum.
It's day to day, and I know you can identify with that. One day you're ahead, the next day you have that weasel Gore wanting to count dimples of people who maybe "intended" to vote for him, and the ones who "briefly contemplated" voting for him but then changed their minds.

My problem was I spent too much money in areas where I shouldn't have (landscaping, buying birds) and not enough in areas where I should have (film supplies).
But!, even in my sinking circumstance, I want to take this opportunity to contribute to your mounting legal fees for the Florida recount.

Like you, I have faith in America, and it's legal system, and know everything will work out, - and in no time at all, we all will be, unshackled, together.

Lazlo Toth

Encl: $2

SWANSON

HUNGRY-MAN

Salisbury Steak

with Mushroom Gravy
Macaroni & Cheese
Green Beans and
Apple Crumb
Dessert

NOW!
50% MORE MEAT
with Macaroni & Cheese

FLORIDA THRILLA!
FIGHT TO THE FINISH
Newsweek®

newsweek.msnbc.com

1624

MR LAZLO TOTH
PO BOX 245
FAIRFAX CA 94978

LAZLO TOTH
Post Office Box 245, Fairfax, California 94978

November 24, 2000

Chief of Operations
Swanson Frozen Hungry Man Dinner Division / Plasit Foods
Executive Campus 6
Cherry Hills, New Jersey 08002-4112

Dear Hungry Man Division Chief,

    I am writing regarding your <u>HUNGRY MAN Saiisbury Steak Dinner.</u> I'll get right to the point - you've got design problems in your packaging arena. Big time.

    I did exactly what I was told to do on the package.
    I REMOVED the plastic covering from the Apple Crumb Desert, and poked holes throughout the green beans.
    I Microwaved on High for 8 minutes, and after the microwave cooled down, I cooked it on HALF POWER more.
    But! when I went to "Stir the Macaroni & Cheese before serving", as instructed, I noticed (who wouldn't?) that the Macaroni & Cheese had melted over (merged) into the Apple Crumb Desert compartment.
    Believe me, It was not a pleasant sight. I could hardly eat it.

    I've been involved recently with the Kimberly - Clarks Corporation in Wisconsin, helping them work out some kinks with their KLEENEX EXPRESSIONS line, and I'd be happy to pitch in and help you hurdle this spill over dilemma.

    The FIRST THING we have to do, IMMEDIATELY!, is switch around the Green Beans with the Apple Crumb Desert. This is no FINAL SOLUTION, but a manuever we should embrace until I can get out there to tour the plants and meet the Chefs.

    <u>I know what you're thinking</u>: If we just SWITCH the Green Beans with the Apple Crumb, won't the Macaroni & Cheese just spill over into the Green Beans then? The answer is YES!, you're right, the Macaroni & Cheese will <u>still</u> melt over to the adjacent compartment, but!, LIKE I SAID, switching around the compartments is just "TEMPORARY", it's not a FINAL move, tell everyone to just CALM DOWN.

    The solution may be as simple as substituting Macaroni and Cheese with APPLESAUCE. This way, if the applesauce erupts over into the Apple Crumb Desert, hardly anybody will be able to tell.

    One thing I know for sure, we've all got to stay upbeat,

Laylo Toth

December 6, 2000

Mr. Lazlo Toth
P.O. Box 245
Fairfax, CA 94978-0245

Dear Mr. Toth:

We are sorry that you were disappointed with your purchase of Swanson®
Hungry-Man® Salisbury Steak Dinner.

We take great pride in the quality of all of our products and consumer
satisfaction is our greatest concern. We thoroughly inspect all
ingredients and containers before use, and carefully monitor each step
of the process. We are committed to providing high quality products.

We've received many requests from other consumers to bring back the
mashed potatoes in our Salisbury Steak Dinner and have made the decision
to eliminate the macaroni and cheese in favor of the potatoes! We
anticipate that supplies of the mashed potato Salisbury Steak Dinner
will be in stores on a nation-wide basis by late September or early
October, 2000.

We will forward your comments to our Quality Management Team so the
Swanson® Hungry-Man® Salisbury Steak Dinner team and other consumers can
benefit from your comments. Thank you!

Enclosed is a coupon for the Vlasic Foods product of your choice.

Sincerely,

Lisa Hird
Consumer Response Representative

LAH/cl

0153243A

LAZLO TOTH
Post Office Box 245. Fairfax. California 94978.

December 14, 2000

President Elect
Governor George W. Bush
Austin, TEXAS

Dear President Elect Bush,

Congradulations!
Finally!,after <u>36 DAYS</u> you are <u>President-Elect George W. Bush</u>.
And 37 DAYS from today, you will be known for all time as Mister PRESIDENT George W. BUSH. Hail to the Chief! Stand.

Your Victory/Reconciliation Speech tonight was outstanding, You really lucked by being able to give your speech one hour after Gore's. I thought after all this time one of you would end being a sore looser and the other one would end being a sore winner, but, you both pulled it off, you could hardly tell.

Gore's "It'S TIME FOR <u>ME</u> TO GO" swan song speech was MOVING. By that I mean that it was one of the few times we got to see <u>both sides</u> of his face <u>MOVING</u> together at the <u>same time</u>, usually they take turns.
To say that he is WOODEN, is an affront to lumber.

They say President Kennedy always carried a piece of paper in his pocket with the number 113,057 written on it. That's the small popular vote margin he won by — he kept the paper in his pocket to help keep him humble.

I suggest that from now on, at all times, you carry a small piece of tree BARK in your pocket.
It will serve as a reminder that YOU WON (in the electoral college), but that more people voted for your opponent than for you, and that your opponent was part <u>TREE</u>.
That should <u>REALLY</u> keep you humble.

It's hard to think of the future when even the PRESENT is behind schedule, but, at this time, I would like to apply for a job in your administration as <u>Personal Assistant to Vice President Cheney</u>. I know I can be of great help to him.

Onward!

Lazlo Toth

Lazlo Toth

DECEMBER 25, 2000/JANUARY 1, 2001 $3.95

PERSON OF THE YEAR

PRESIDENT-ELECT
GEORGE W. BUSH

Laura and I thank you so much for your kind words. This was an historic, unprecedented election. Now that it is over, I am confident that we, as a nation, can put our differences aside and work together in a spirit of bipartisan cooperation to do what is in the best interest of all our citizens.

I look forward to the challenges ahead with great anticipation and with deep respect for the office entrusted to me by the American people. Laura and I are grateful for the opportunity to serve our country by calling upon the very best in each of us as Americans.

[signature]

PAID FOR BY BUSH-CHENEY PRESIDENTIAL TRANSITION FOUNDATION INC. NOT PAID FOR AT TAXPAYERS EXPENSE.

PRESIDENT-ELECT
GEORGE W. BUSH

AND NOW, THE HARD PART

December 15, 2000
<u>You went down swingin', just like Vito Antufermo</u>.

Lazlo Toth
Post Office Box 245
Fairfax, California 94978

Vice President Al Gore
Washington, D.C.

Dear Vice President Gore,

Cheer Up! You have a right to be bumbed out about loosing the Presidency, but it's not like you didn't get the most votes!

Be Positive!   Stop saying that you're already thinking about running again in 2004. People are going to think you have nothing else to do. Tell them you have been mauling around the future in your mind, but the going is slow because you have so many options.

I. <u>DENTAL SCHOOL</u>
By going to Dental School, you will show the nation that you have the guts to take on a whole new career. Also, you will make history again! for being the "FIRST Vice President of the U.S. to go to Dental School after he left Office".
If you start right away (JANUARY), and go summers, you could complete your DDS in time to still run for President in 2004.
And, just IF, you should fail to get enough votes in the electoral college <u>again</u>, at least this time you'll have a profession to fall back on, and your dental school alumni organization to give you support.

2. <u>BEN AND JERRY'S</u>
I read in the paper that their new CEO is not working out and they're looking for a new one. I can see you working for them, they like the environment, too. Check it out. Go to your web.

3. <u>OTHER COMPANIES</u>
 Make a list of your favorite companies, look up their numbers in the phone book, then call them and ask for the address of where to send your resume.

Good Luck!

Lazlo Toth

Lazlo Toth

DEMOCRATIC NATIONAL COMMITTEE

January 16, 2001

Mr. Lazlo Toth
PO Box 245
Fairfax, CA 94978

Dear Lazlo,

None of us could have ever imagined the historic events that have transpired in the last month. We want to take this opportunity to thank you for your support of the Gore/Lieberman Recount Committee. Since November 7th, we have fought together to give the American public the voice that it deserves and our democracy demands.

Your steadfast committment and genorsity throughout our journey together has been incredible. In the last two years, you have repeatedly answered the Democratic call to action willingly and wholeheartedly. We have truly become a family fighting side by side for those issues important to all Americans.

We are extremely grateful for the outpouring of support from Democrats throughout the nation for our efforts in Florida and we look forward to continuing to work together. Again, you have our heartfelt thanks.

Sincerely,

Al Gore

Joe Lieberman

Democratic Party Headquarters ■ 430 South Capitol Street, SE ■ Washington, DC, 20003 ■ (202) 863-8000 ■ Fax (202) 863-8174
Paid for by the Democratic National Committee. Contributions to the Democratic National Committee are not tax deductible.
Visit our website at www.democrats.org.

December 14, 2000

Chief Justice William Rhinquist
United States Supreme Court
Washington. D. C.

Lazlo Toth
Post Office Box 245
Fairfax, California 94978

Dear Chief Justice Rhinquist,

On behalf of a partially grateful public, I would like to thank you for stepping in, and putting an end, to the 2000 Presidential election.

Thanks to you, and the other Republican appointed supreme court justices, the fate of the Nation is no longer in the hands of Florida Citrus Merchants, but back in the hands of those with a more worldly vision – Texas Oil Men.

But, I'm not writing to you now inregard to our mutual interest in the Law, my concerns are of a more retail nature.

I write regarding the robe you wear, with the 4 gold stripes "Boldly Adorned" on each sleeve.

I read (PEOPLE MAGAZINE) that it was modeled after one worn by an actor in a play you went to see, called <u>IOLANTHE</u>, by Gilbert and Sullivan, and that's how you came up with the idea.

My idea is similar to yours, but!, in TERRYCLOTHE.

The product name: **THE SUPREME BATH ROBE.**
<u>Texture (strength):</u> – lo% Thicker than a medium weight bathtowel.
  Arms: Four gold stripes "Internationally" Hand Sewn on each sleeve.
      Adorned midway between the elbow and the armpit.
  Business Plan: The goal of maximum profit can be obsceened by using inexpensive thread, and by teaming up with a labor force in a third world country, who sew in their own homes or huts.

Your Honor, on the horizon, I see odor of a possible conflict.

Once we're in K-Mart, and Macy's, and all the other fine stores and catalogs, common logic tells me, GILBERT or SULLIVAN, or somebody else from the play, is going to find out . And IF they charge ME, in a court of law, with misappropriatingly stealing their robe design, - If ! I have to go under oath, I've got to tell the "whole truth", and the whole truth is, I got the whole idea from <u>YOU</u>.

How could I "STEAL" <u>Gilbert and Sullivan's robe idea</u>, when I never even saw the play! I can't even pronounce it! And, I don't want to. I don't like plays. They're too long.

<u>Future's Blueprint</u>: By facing this looming accusation "Pre Post Facto", we establish the beginning of a paper trail, which down the line will proove, beyond a witness of a doubt, that I never even saw the play, and that we both were aware of it. And! that I had no idea whatsoever! that Gilbert and Sullivan's robe had gold stripes on the sleeves just like my bathrobes.

I was under the impression the whole time that you thought up the gold stripes idea by yourself, I wasn't even there.

I am not a lawyer, but my Father wanted me to go to Law School,

Lazlo Toth

MEET

RANDY

The
Robot
Altar
Boy

- CAN WALK DOWN AISLE FOR PROCESSIONS

- CAN POUR WINE (BUT! <u>NEVER DRINKS IT</u>).

- CAN HOLD A LIT CANDLE.

- <u>NEVER LATE</u>

- CAN ONLY MOVE ON FLAT SURFACES
   (IMPOSSIBLE to take on CAMPING TRIPS)

- Can SAVE $Millions on Insurance
   (Has NO MEMORY — only batteries)

December 24, 2000

President
Mars Candy Company, INC.   07840-1503
Hackettstown, New Jersey

 Mr. Lazlo Toth
P.O. Box 245
Fairfax, CA 94978

Dear Sir:

I am happy to report the wonderful news that I have won your $2 Million Contest!

I have found the red M&M with two M's" on it! I have been eating your candy almost on a weekly basis, checking each piece, and with only ONE WEEK LEFT in the year, finally VICTORY! Thank you.

I know these things take time to settle, and it may be weeks before I get my main check, and I was wondering if I can have some kind of an advance until we settle up.
If I could have $10,000 as soon as possible, before the end of the calendar year, that would be fine.

After I receive the advance, I would like to have the remaining One Million Nine Hundred and Ninety nine thousand Dollars, in one lump sum, instead of having taxes deducted. I have a lot of expenses I can write off this year,and my deductions may make withholding unneccessary and complicate matters for no good reason.

The money comes at a moment when my busines (film studio) is/was facing some financial hardship, and utility consequences, but not any more! Thanks to you, M&M's, my favorite candy of all time!

Thank you for making all this possible,

Lazlo Toth

Lazlo Toth

P.S. I am sending my "Double M" M&M wrapped in Reynold's Aluminum Foil to secure its safety, and so it will be able to MELT IN YOUR BANK, NOT IN THE MAIL, do you get that one?

a division of Mars, Incorporated
High Street, Hackettstown, New Jersey 07840 • Telephone 908-852-1000

January 10, 2001

Mr. Lazlo Toth
P.O. Box 245
Fairfax, CA 94978

Dear Mr. Toth:

Thank you for your letter advising us that you believe you are the winner of the "M&M's"® Millennium Promotion.

This promotion ended on December 1, 1998 with a confirmed winner. Only one wrapper was created for the Grand Prize winner. The requirement for winning, as stated on the wrapper, was the official game piece which is printed on the inside of the wrapper. The game piece indicated if you were an "Instant Winner" and what you won.

We hope you will continue to enjoy future promotions with M&M/MARS products.

Sincerely,

Gloria E. Vivenzio
Consumer Affairs

MANUFACTURERS COUPON

Expiration Date: 07/31/02

To: Mr. Lazlo Toth

Please accept this coupon with our compliments. It entitles you to the following:

One FREE 16oz. (or less) package of any M&M/MARS confectionery product

CONSUMER: Limit one coupon per package as indicated. You pay sales tax. Void if altered, transferred, sold, reproduced or exchanged.

RETAILER: M&M/MARS will reimburse you for the face value of this coupon plus $.08 handling if submitted in compliance with M&M/MARS Coupon Redemption Policy - #M1, available upon request, incorporated here-in by reference. Redeemable only in the U.S.A. or U.S. government installations. Void where prohibited, taxed or restricted by law. Cash value 1/100 of one cent. Send coupons to: M&M/MARS, P.O. Box 880-622, El Paso, TX 88588-0622. ©Mars, Incorporated 1998.

1790679A GEV

Retail Price _____   40000 135810

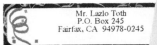
Police: Woman beat sister with telephone

LORAIN — A 24-year-old Lorain woman who is accused of beating her sister with a telephone was arrested for felonious assault after she said her sister deserved it for yanking the phone out of the wall while she was talking on it, police said.

Jennifer Burchell of 1336 Narragansett Drive pleaded innocent in Lorain Municipal Court to a charge of felonious assault, according to court records. While awaiting a preliminary hearing on the charge, Ms. Burchell was released on a $1,000 bond.

Officers responded to the Narragansett home early yesterday morning to find the 24-year-old victim bleeding from a cut on her head, police said. The woman was taken to Lorain Community/St. Joseph Regional Health Center where she was treated for the wound, police said.

Before she left for the hospital, the victim told officers her sister hit her with a white General Electric push button phone when she asked if she could use it, police said.

After the alleged assault, the suspect left the home, police said. Officers arrested the suspect after finding her walking near Oberlin Avenue and Tower Boulevard. She allegedly admitted beating her sister and told officers her sister deserved it for pulling the phone out of the wall.

The phone, which had blood and hair stuck to it, was confiscated as evidence, according to a police report.

Jeffery Immell
Chief Executive Officer
General Electric Company
3135 Easton Turnpike
Fairfield, Conn. 06431

Dear Chief Immell,

Congratulations on reaching the top at GE.
WATT a way to start 2001!
Although the exact amount of your pay package is yet to be announced, former CEO Jack Welch, who you are replacing, pocketed $61 million in 1999, so it's clear you've slipped into a very suede spot.

I'm sure GE's famous founder, Thomas A. Edison, who was born less than fifty miles from Lorain, Ohio, the town where the unsisterly incident mentioned in this newspaper article took place, is cheering for you in his grave, although I am not sure where exactly he is buried.

Although there was no controlling legal authority that said Vice President Albert Gore shouldn't have made unsolicited telephone calls from his White House Office, the press didn't drag the name of the manufacturer of the telephone he shouldn't have been using into the mess! When Linda Tripp taped Monica Lewinski's calls, the color of the phone she used was never mentioned! Why did they let Tripp's telephone off the hook, but, for no apparent reason, name the model and color of the General Electric telephone the sister used in this sordid situation?

Yes!, it was a White, Push Button telephone that was involved, but wouldn't hair and blood stick to other models, besides the white, push button one, if the impact of the phone on her sister's scull was of a similar magnitude?
And, face it, it's not just true just for telephones! The same thing could happen if somebody got hit in the head with one or more of a lot of the other products you make. Fans, Toasters, and Light Bulbs, are just a few examples that come to mind, and that's enough.

I know you're brand new in there, and there's no way you should be blamed or made to feel responsible for the pain inflicted on every person in America who has been on the flesh side of one of your products, but as the <u>new</u> CEO, I hope you'll try to stop this kind of thing from happening again, by ordering your factory managers in the Phillipines, where I understand you make your White Push Button model, to switch to a larger, stronger, better quality Wall Screw, so that this type of injury, that happened when Welsh was in there, won't ever happen again.

Sir, I'm taking a survey of CEO's, and this is the question:
In American Business, what do you think is said more often?
How can we make this product better? OR , How can we make this product cheaper?

Lazlo Toth

⚡ THOMSON CONSUMER ELECTRONICS

P.O. Box 6127, Mail Stop INH 815, Indianapolis, IN 46206-6127, USA
Tel: 1(317) 415-4151 • Fax: 1(317) 415-2625
Internet Address: http://www.nipper.com

March 14, 2001

M. Lazlo Toth
PO BOX 245
FAIRFAX, CA 94978 0245

Dear M. Toth:

Thank you for your inquiry concerning the design and quality of your product.

Consumer satisfaction is very important to us and we continually strive to provide the best consumer electronic products available. We invest substantial resources in market research to develop products that meet consumer needs and expectations.

We are continually finding ways to improve reliability, designs, product quality, and professional service.

Your comments are appreciated and we thank you for taking your valuable time to contact us.

Sincerely,

Gina Smith

Consumer Relations Coordinator

Model Number:
Serial Number:
Date Of Purchase:
Your File Number: 2643085

John F. Welch Jr., the former G.E. chief, discusses his retirement perks on TV.

$357,128 Amount retired General Electric CEO Jack Welch receives each month from his GE pension, according to an affidavit filed as part of his divorce proceedings

January 16. 2 0 0 1

G. E. Vivenzio
Department of Consumers Affairs
M&M's Division / Mars Incorporated
Hackettstown, New Jersey, 07840

Mr. Lazlo Toth
P.O. Box 245
Fairfax, CA 94978

Dear Consumers Affairs Officer Vivenzio,

I looked closer at the M&M's "Instantly Win $2,000,000" wrapper, and it's PLAIN, that I must have misinterupted some of meaning of some of the wording on some of the wrapper. Sometimes, I don't know what's wrong with me.

So clearly it say's, *"Look for the Millennium candles " mm," and you may have the winning Wrapper".*

I think what threw me off was the combination of the Words with the Art on the wrapper. The words - "Look f o r the Millinium Candies". next to the art work (picture) of the little red m&m, - I thought they went together.

I think that's the reason I misled myself into thinking that "Look for the Candies" meant that if I found one inside with "mm on it, like the red one on the WRAPPER, I could be an INSTANT WINNER. I feel like such a fool.

But, still, I can't help but wonder, - IF the winning " mm" is inside on the wrapper, why do you ask people to "LOOK for the Candies?" L O O K for the candies" for w h a t? L o o k FOR the candies to know if you have a winning WRAPPER? It doesn't make sense! Not if, in order to be an INSTANT WINNER, you have to LOOK INSIDE the WRAPPER, to see if the "official game piece" is PRINTED inside.

And whoever heard of a Game PIECE being PRINTED? Correct me if I'm wrong, but, to me, a "piece" is something you should be able to hold in your hand, not something PRINTED on a wrapper!

AND!, Why does it say, on the wrapper,"No Purchase necessary". The "Details on the Back" say, "TO PLAY: Look inside wrapper for official game message". How can you look INSIDE the wrapper, If you don't purchase it first? Do you think any grocery store in their right mind is going to let you TEAR OPEN the pack, pour the M& M's out on the counter, turn the wrapper inside out to look INSIDE, and if the GAME PIECE is not PRINTED inside, let you scotch tape it all back together and put it back on the shelf? For one thing, I think that violates health codes.

But, hygiene aside, please just answer me this:
- W H Y would "The Official Candy of the Millennium" end it's "Millenium Promotion" one year BEFORE the millennium even began? A n d....
- H o w you can say "NO PURCHASE NECESSARY", when you have to open the package and look INSIDE to find out if you won?

Help me understand how you can INSTANTLY WIN $2,000,000 without buying the candy?

Lazlo Toth

a division of Mars, Incorporated
High Street, Hackettstown, New Jersey 07840 • Telephone 908-852-1000

February 2, 2001

Mr. Lazlo Toth
P.O. Box 245
Fairfax, CA 94978

Dear Mr. Toth:

Thank you for your follow-up letter concerning our Millennium Promotion.
I hope to clarify your inquiries.

M&M/MARS has many promotions for its products. Scheduling can be
difficult, as well as constraining. This promotion was intended to be a
"hype" for the new millennium. So, it ended prior to the actual turn of
the century.

Indicated on the front of your wrapper, in the lower left hand corner,
printed instructions direct you to look on the back of the wrapper. On
the back of the wrapper are instructions for where to write to obtain
free game pieces without purchasing the product.

If you have any further questions, please call us at 1-800-222-0293 from
8:30 AM to 5:00 PM, Monday through Friday, EST.

Sincerely,

Gloria E. Vivenzio
Consumer Affairs

GEV/cl 1790679B

KNIGHTS OF SERRA
Gran Grupo Central du Nord
Pius XI Branch / Baja Alberta-Petaluma
POB 245 Fairfax. California 94978 U.S.A.

<u>January 21, 2001</u>

<u>Branch Chief</u>
LAZLO TOTH

Prefetto Pietro Cardinale PALAZZINI
SACRED DEPARTMENT for the CAUSES of SAINTS
Vatican City, (STATE)

Your Eminence,

Today! a Nun who was told by physicians that there was <u>no known cure</u> for the Lupus she suffered, and another Nun, diagnosed with SCOLIOSIS (curviture of the spine), are now, TODAY!, walking around San Francisco LIKE GAZELLES - with <u>no remaining remnants</u> of curviture of the spine, or LUPUS whatsoever.

They stand as straight as stalks of corn,- their spines like Totem Poles! WHY? Because of PRAYERS to Father Junipero Serra (and Posture Cream) - <u>not</u> SURGERY!

Years ago the Vatican asked for <u>Proof</u>. We mailed you XRAY's of one of the Nuns curved and then restored spine, as well as medical records (from 9 Doctors) for Sister Carmelita Brotellone, the Lupus carrier.

And what do we get back from Rome in return? No letter! An embossed POSTCARD? No! Not even confirmation that you received our package of medical PROOF!

Cardinal!, do you think that's anyway to run a SACRED Department of Miracles? I don't think so. What is the problem? WHY! do we get NO HELP WHATSOEVER swimming the chunky waters towards the port of justifiable Sainthood?

WHY! won't the Pope hear our plea? Do we have to have Blessed Junipero Serra's profile embossed on cabbage rolls and have a blimp drop them into St. Peter's square to get some attention for our cause?

NOW! there is word that the Pope wants to make his two favorites — Mother Teresa and Padre Pio SAINTS!

Padre Pio just died in 1989!

Cardinal!, Fr. Serra has been dead since 1784! How do you think this makes us feel?

And how many miracles does the moody recluse have to his name besides Lola Falana and the nut case fighter pilot who say's Fr. Pio appearded to him in his B-52?

Counting them, exactly ZERO in my opinion!

And Mother Teresa, who some say was a KGB Mole, has ZERO miracles as well, But! <u>ONE</u> PENDING, big deal.

Lupus! Scoliosis! Do these CURES mean nothing to you Europeans?

Prefetto!, the last straw has entered the barn! I suggest your committee <u>FIND THOSE X-rays</u> and make Fr. Serra a Saint NEXT!, before California Catholics are forced to take their dream of a California Saint to the altar of the Greek Orthodox Church, or even the <u>Episcopalians</u>, and start the schism no Roman Catholic desires. *TOTH* 3<u>RD</u> degree Knight

ANCHE LOLA FALANA
E' UNA DEVOTA DI PADRE PIO

VALLWURM AND DWARVDOBLE
ATTORNEYS AT LAW

<u>Founders/Partners</u>
Albert W. Vallwurm
George Dwarfdouble

Wyler W. Vallwurm
Associate

Hon. David Kendal   2- 0- 2 347-0119 . 2- 2- 2 001
C/o President Clinton Defence Fund Headquarters
1010 Vermont
Washington, D.C. 20005

Lazlo Toth
P.O. Box 245
Fairfax, California
94930 U.S.A.

Dear Mr. Kendal,

Congradulations on your victory representing President Clinton, and resolving, once and for all, on his last day in office, his looming litigation resulting from his testimony in the Lewinski case, for being "at varience with the truth", or for, what most Americans call "Lieing under Oath" <u>You</u> got him off with a sentence of - having his <u>law licence taken away for 5 years</u>. I call that – GENIUS! Big time! Stand up!

If, please!, you feel a challenge to pilot a similar mission, in a low lucrative, less profile arena, my case begs you to extend your talents.

First let me tell you a little something about my linkage to the stationary of this firm. I found it in the desk I let Wyler (Willie) Vallwurm use while he was involved on a project at my former film studio, TOTHWORKS.
I first met Willie about 2 years ago. He wanted to make a movie about his dreams. He was going to play all the parts, in all the dreams, and his Mother (the daughter of the inventor of Bouillon Cubes) had agreed to finance it. Bottom line? I had a lot of very pricey landscaping going on at the lot at the time, and, didn't budget in enough money for some basic supplies, and to cut to the short of it, I'm not even in the film business anymore - it's a rat race.
Looking back, the first thing I felt, when reading the "DREAM ON WILLIE" script, was sorry for the paper it was written on. I don't know why anyone would want to try to remember, let alone try to "recreate" boring "dreams" like his. But, I had bills to pay, and he even agreed to invest in my studio, besides agreeing to the DREAM budget I figured up.

I just don't understand why <u>making</u> a film isn't joyful enough on its own, and why so much emphasis is put on <u>watching</u> it? Why does eveyone have to stretch things out nowdays? We shot it, that's what counts!, but, all they just keep asking about is, "the <u>missing footage</u>".
Why don't they ever talk about the "<u>missing plot</u>" !
If you could have only witnessed Willie playing "Himself in 3 years" in a "<u>Dream from the Future</u>", you would agree with me that the way I chose to shoot the scene, as well as other scenes, was the right way - using a camera unincombered by film stock.

Sometimes <u>NOTHING</u> is <u>BETTER</u> than Something!
I think that's the approach we should take, - it's kind of a ZEN DEFENCE, and with the trial taking place in San Francisco, there's a good chance we can get some ZEN- BUDDESTS on the Jury, and you can get me off with just having to take some Accounting classes,, or something like that.

PLEASE take my case!, I don't know what I'm going to do without you.
But if you can't, I know you must still be pretty busy, mopping things up, - I was hoping maybe you could you please tell me where I can contact <u>F. Lee Bailey</u>, he's my second choice after you.

Lazlo Toth

Lazlo Toth
POET IN RESIDENCE
#245 **CalIfornIa** 94978

January 15, 2001

Bush-Cheney Presidential Transition Foundation
Transition Employment Center
1616 Anderson Rd. McLean, VA. 22102

Dear President-elect Bush,

I just heard about your decision <u>not</u> to appoint a
new Poet Laureat as part of your administration, and that no
one will read, not even ONE! Poem, at your inauguaration.
The reason?   They said you want to keep the ceremony SHORT,
that's why you cut us Poets out, because you "want to keep it
short".

I see no rhyme or reason why your barely budding
quasi-ligitimate administration has gone out of its way to
drop the nobel post of POET LAUREAT and reject POETRY as part
of the inauguration ceremony. Especially since you
imphasised EDUCATION so greatly in your campaign.

W h y ? Longefellow ! Why Whittier !
Corso. F r o s t ! , Beecher. Stow !,
 A l l !   S t a b b e d   in   the
 B aa c k .
W h y W h y?

I beg you, for your own sake, to reconsider your
short sighted decision, and accept my proposal whos primary
purpose is to accommodate your time constrains..

Mister President, Elect, for your ceremony, I have
written <u>the shortest Inaugural poem in HIstory</u>, it is only
TWO WORDS long. And!, if even at this length, you feel it
still "too long", and would "take up too much time", I have
figured out a plan and am willing to edit further, as much as
to up to half it's original length. Yes! HALF! Because!,
even then, STILL!, it can <u>maintain</u> it's basic <u>theme</u> without
losing the <u>core</u> of it's <u>message</u>.

Furthermore!, I am willing to work my entire four years
as Poet Laureat for FREE, without any salary, and personally
pay for my own tax deductable poetry supplies.
But!, to supplement my salaryless position, I would be
willing to work a second shift, at a living wage, as a
special Assistant to Vice President Cheney. I can be of
great help to him.

I am ready to chip in and get rolling,

Lazlo Toth

Lazlo Toth

BUSH CHENEY

Bush-Cheney 2000

News & Info

Issues

Get Involved

Contribute

Toolbox

Ho

Bush-Cheney Transition Site

presidential inaugural committee

ophy
ief is
great
this
ens
le—
any
ent
'Go
hild
city'
ove
ay."

Above: Jan. 20, 2001. George W. Bush is sworn in as the 43rd U.S. President by Chief Justice William Rehnquist (r). Between them are his daughter Jenna and wife, Laura. Left: Days later, the new President visits Merritt Elementary School in Washington, D.C.

HANDS

000, Inc. P

TOtH LAZLo \
box 245 fairfax, california. 94978

February 19

To: Mr. J. D. Salinger
    Cornish, N. H.

Dear Mr. Salinger,
        I read about the woman who recently sold , FOR PUBLICATION, the
love letters you wrote her twenty years ago, because she "needed the
money to send her children to college". They say Judas had kids who
waited too long to apply for scholarships, too.

        Recently, in a similar vain, the swimming porkroast, Ester
Williams, was on the Larry King Show, promoting her "tell-all" book, -
spilling secrets, telling intimate tales about private times she
claims she shared with famous men in her life, (Ricardo Maltibaum,
Jeff Chandler, Johnny Puleo and the Harmonicats, Etc.), - ridiculing
them, betraying their trust, munching on the mulch of their fading
fame.

        BUT!, <u>this is the best part</u> - when Larry asks her, "How old are
you?" she seems offended he would ask her age, and replies, "That's
private". She doesn't seem to feel that there's anything "private"
about telling Larry about the time she walked into her bedroom and
found Jeff Chandler wearing one of her gowns. Doesn't she think Jeff
Chandler, may think that's kind of "private"?, and that maybe it's
UNFAIR because he's dead and can't tell His side of the story, which
is probably that he probably never even liked her, and the only reason
he was attracted to her <u>at all</u>, was because she had such large
shoulders, and she was one of the few women in Hollywood at the time
who's gowns fit him.
        She didn't mention that MOE, one of the Three Stooges, once said
that he'd "rather have sex with Farm Animals than with Ester Williams
again", because, he said, "at least they don't fake it".

<u>Change the subject:</u>
        The article said you continue to write, but you don't care about
publishing anything. It said when you finish writing a book, you
just wrap it up and put it in a <u>safe.</u>.
        Now, I'm starting to feel the same way you do. I understand
perfectly.

        My new basic philosophy: <u>It's the journey, not the burger.</u>
        I'm not going to get upset with any of them ever again, I will
stay calm, and to guarantee myself this promise, I've made a vow not to
talk on the phone to <u>anyone</u>, especially during daylight hours.

        Mr. Salinger, I now have three books ready to put into storage.
But! my problem,
I don't have a SAFE of my own, and instead of me having to go out and
buy some expensive new millenium Y2M fireproof Safe, my hope is you
might be willing to spare some small space, for my books, on a shelf in
<u>your</u> safe.

        They say when people write to you, you never answer their letters
- that's one of the things I like about you. But, I'm willing to
gamble and take your answer as "YES", and when my books arrive, if you
don't want to put them in your safe, and want to just throw them in
your garbage can instead, that's fine, too, because, for all
I know, you could have put them in your safe instead.

Lazlo Toth

HAROLD OBER ASSOCIATES

INCORPORATED

Telephone
(212) 759-8600

Fax Number
(212) 759-9428

425 MADISON AVENUE, NEW YORK, N.Y. 10017

February 27, 2001

Lazlo Toth
P.O. Box 245
Fairfax, CA 94978-0245

Dear Mr. Toth,

I'm responding to your recent letter to J.D. Salinger. It would be appreciated if you did not send Mr. Salinger any books as proposed in the last two paragraphs in your letter.

Thank you and I'm sorry to disappoint you.

Sincerely,

Phyllis Westberg

PW/kg

LAZLO TOTH
CALIFORNIA

February 6, 2001

Mr. Albert Gore
Columbia University
New York, New York

Dear Al,

Congratulations on being accepted into Columbia.

From what everything I've read, it's one of the top schools on the east coast, and I wish you all the luck in the world with your classes.

Lazlo Toth

Lazlo Toth

March 5, 2001

Mr. Lazio Toth
P.O. Box 245
Fairfax, CA 94978

Dear Ms. Toth:

Thank you for your warm letter welcoming me to the teaching profession at Columbia University. I sincerely appreciation your friendship and support as I begin this new endeavor.

Education is the cornerstone upon which success, innovation, and discovery are based. American can be a high-growth, high-wage nation, but only if our people possess high-quality skills that prepare them for the competitive demands of the 21st Century. I am proud to have the opportunity to share my knowledge and to participate in such a vital and esteemed profession.

Again, thank you for writing. I wish you all the best.

Sincerely,

Al Gore

March 31, 2001

Swanson Hungry-Man Salisbury Steak Dinner Team
C/o Lisa Hird
Consumer Response Representative
Vlasic Foods (SWANSONS) International
Cherry Hills, N.J. 08002-4112

LAZLO TOTH
Post Office Box 245, Fairfax, California 94978

Dear Lisa,

Your guys are doing a great job!

Eliminating the Macaroni and Cheese in favor of mashed potatoes, not only hurdled the Macaroni and Cheese spill (boil) over delema, but was a brilliant cullinary decision as well.

Maybe it's just my visual deception, but I feel that besides the fact that the mashed potatoes don't invade the green beans, like the Macaroni and Cheese did, to me, the mashed potatoes even seem to make the sliced mushrooms atop the salisbury steak taste even more pleantifull!

I suggested APPLE SAUCE instead of Macaroni and Cheese - shows you what I know!

But now, - FORWARD!, - I present to you - A N e w I d e a !

An idea that can LAUNCH the Swanson Hungry-Man Salisbury Steak Dinner Team into the future of frozen food history.

An idea that LEAPS the boundries of single species dining- and branches out to embrace household pets.

I present to you.....

HUNGRY FRIENDS
INTERSPECIES MICROWAVE DINNERS.

A compact, culinary medley of SURF (Bits 'o Cod) and TURFs (salisbury steak and Liver saute) designed exclusively for the ONE HUMAN, ONE CAT, ONE DOG household.

A delicious three sepecies, three entre meal, conviently packed into ONE foot long container. All you have to do is MIRCORWAVE ON HIGH FIVE MINUTES, and - what do you get? You get O N E very happy household, AND! a meals medly that not only enhanses (quality) dinner time companionship, - but! saves ENERGY (dishwasher), and meal preparation TIME, as well.

I think the secret to a successful launch of such an unchartered concept will be greatly enhanced if we had a celebrity spokesman -

My numer ONE Choice - Prince Charles of England.

I think we may have a shot at getting him because he may see this as a way to help thaw his families negative image in the man-animal friendship arena, and at the same time, enhanse his own popularity by being associated with a unique, upscale product such as ours, instead of his present female companion, that nobody seems to like very much.

Plus! it also lets him be seen as " just a regular guy", who sometimes has dinner with his pets, instead of with her.

Laylo

April 25, 2001

Ms Toth
P. O. Box 245
Fairfax, CA 94978

Dear Ms Toth:

Thank you for contacting us regarding your idea for Vlasic Foods. We appreciate your interest in our products.

In an effort to continually improve our products, the marketing, advertising and research and development staff at Vlasic Foods International work with a variety of external agencies and consultants. We are constantly evaluating our products, packaging, advertising and marketing programs. In order to avoid misunderstandings with members of the public who wish to submit ideas for possible new products, packaging, advertising or marketing concepts, we do not review ideas submitted from individuals.

We are sorry that we could not give you a more positive reply, but want to thank you for your interest in Vlasic, and wish you the best of luck in the future.

Sincerely,

Coutanyer Evans
Consumer Response Representative

CIE/VLA

0179286A

SAY YEAH   STAND BY ME   pLEASE

Opening of Former President Clinton's

HARLEM
OFFICE
7-30-01

thank you
congressman charlie
Rangel thank
you Senator shu

When the Night has come July 30, 2001

I was there
for you. You
were there for
me. TOGETHER
let's be
there TOGETHER
for me,
SAY YEAH!
I don't care if
the moon is
the only
light we'll
see. Say
Yeah!

SAY YEAH!
PLEASE SAY YEAH!
charlie! charlie, tell
them to say YEAH!
pLease.

July 30, 2001

Former President Bill Clinton
Harlem Headquarters
Harlem New York

Dear President Clinton,

"Stand By Me" was a terrible choice of song for you to use as
your theme for the opening ceremony of your new Harlem offices.

It's a song about a man who has lost it all, someone desperately
begging for assistance.
"When the night has come" it begins, and I wonder, do you consider
this "the night" of your life?
Then, "I won't cry if you stand by me". CRY? Grow up!
Think of all the perks you get, like Free Postage, and Bodyguards to
carry your suitcases.

A much better song would have been The Dell's classic, "Stay in
my Corner".

It's a song that also, lyrically, asks for support, BUT, unlike
STAND BY ME, which all about ME ME ME , Stay in my Corner gives
something back!
"If you stay in my corner, I'll make you oh! so proud."
It say's, "we can empower each other". I'm not here because I have
nowhere else to go.

BUT an even better song would have been HANDY MAN by
Jimmy Jones, and later by James Taylor.
Instead of pleading , "Please... stand by me.", the main thing
HANDY MAN has to say is ,"I'm here for YOU".   And not just sometimes,
no, "I'm with you "24 hours a day".
Instead of TAKING, it's a song about GIVING.
It say's "gather round, I FIX things", I'm not broken, I'm STRONG.
It say's "Tell all your friends, I'm the man to see", I'm here because
I want to help you – NOT "I'm here because they won't let me rent
offices UPTOWN, and you're my last refuge, but " I won't cry" if you
would just let
me crash on your couch for a few nights, then I'll dissappear, and go off
and make speeches for loads of money.

I'm sending you a few SWIZZLE STICKS from my collection as as
office warming present. Don't worry, I washed them,

And let me put an idea in your ear.
Question: What are you going to do when your wife is President?
Answer: Become Mayor of New York. You heard it here first.

Lazlo Toth

Congressman Gary Condit
Modesto, California

8-28-01

U.S. Address:
P.O. Box 245
Fairfax, CA 94978

Dear Conressman Condid,
        WHAT! does Connie Chung have against you!
        You'd think she was one of those airline stewerdess
that you dumped, the way she acts.
        But, you sure left her eating YOUR dust. She's
probaly still at the dry cleaners getting martenized.

    In my opinion, after how well you did in last nights
interview, you'll win re-election to congress , EASY! And I
bet they'll even be talk of you taking over Diane Fienstein's
Senate seat when SHE gets named Ambassador to China.
        I mostly advise political candidates in South America,
that's my specialty, but I'm hoping you may want to to get
together while I'm in the States to talk about me helping out
on your campaign.
        Bill Clinton made a big mistake using STAND BY ME as
the song to open up his Harlem Headquarters, but I would
consider it if I was in your position. You've done a lot for
the Valley, and the agriculture sector, and if they elect a
new Congressman, you think he's goiing to push for Asparagus
tariffs like you can? No way. They should be reminded, -
you stand by me, I'll stand by you!
        Another good campaign song, if you want to face the
Sandra Levi issue head on would be HAVE YOU SEEN HER by the
ChiLights.
        It would show you're interested in finding her, and at the
same time it implys that you don't know where she is either.
        At the beginning it goes, "A MONTH AGO TODAY, I WAS
HAPPY AS A LARK". I would change that to the lengths of
time it's been since she went missing, and to a bird that's
common in your home district.
        For instance, "THREE MONTHS AGO TODAY, I WAS HAPPY AS
A HAWK.

        THE COMMERCIAL could show you asking people if they've
seen her, and towards the end, you should talk straight into
the camera and say: HAVE YOU SEEN HER? I HAVN'T EITHER.
                BUT, WE'REGONNA FIND HER!

        THEN, you give a THUMBS UP, and the song "SEARCHIN'
by the COASTERS begins, as you get into your car, and drive
off to SEARCH for her.
        I know it will be expensive commercial paying for the
rights to two songs, but I think it's worth it.

        If any of this interest you, drop me a line and we'll
set up a pow-wow.

        Fazlo Toth

Mr. Lazlo Toth
P.O. Box 245
Fairfax, CA 94978

12- 2 1 - 01

President David W. Johnson
Campbell Soup Company
Chicken Noodle Division
Camden, N.J. 08103-1799

Dear President Johnson,

I got the letter you had Susan Baranowsky write, telling me that even though your <u>New! Chicken Noodle Soup</u> contains 20% more chicken, the noodle portion remains the same.

She didn't say what the "20% more chicken" replaced, but, I tried the <u>NEW! 20% More Chicken Noodle Soup</u>, and you have won me over!
M'mmm good.

Maybe it's because I was expecting less of them, but, the amount of noodles seems not to have been reduced, just like she said in her letter. But, it's what she didn't say that interests me.

The mystery remains -   How did you do it?
What did you take out of the soup, when you put 20% more chiken into it?   I know it's not the noodles, I have that in writing! But, - what is it? What went?

I don't think it's out of line for someone who has eaten your soup for a lifetime without asking any questions, up till now, to want to know what you took out of the soup when you put 20% more chicken in.

Also, where do you get your chickens?
And what do you do with all the (20% more) feathers?

Thank you very much,

Lazlo Toth

Lazlo Toth

Campbell Soup Company

March 13, 2002

Mr. Lazlo Toth
P. O. Box 245
Fairfax, CA 94978

Dear Mr. Toth:

Thank you for taking the time to contact our President to share your comments about our Campbell's Chicken Noodle Soup. We greatly appreciate your enthusiasm for both our company and our products.

Campbell's Chicken Noodle Soup is America's Favorite Condensed Soup! To create the flavor that everyone knows and loves, Campbell's uses only the finest ingredients, such as freshly prepared noodles, chicken meat, and stock. First, we fill the cans with our fresh famous noodles and broth. Then we add the tender chicken meat to our savory chicken broth. Finally, the can is sealed and thermally processed for safe storage on your shelf.

When we changed our recipe to include 20% more chicken, the quantity of chicken was the only change that was made; all other ingredients remained the same. As you can see, Campbell Soup Company takes pride in the quality of our soups. It is our belief that the consumer deserves nothing less than the finest ingredients in the soups they demand. Once again, we appreciate your feedback and we hope that this information was helpful to you.

Sincerely,

Susan Baranowsky

Susan Baranowsky
Manager - Consumer Response Center
1058539C

CONSUMER RESPONSE AND INFORMATION CENTER • CAMDEN, NEW JERSEY 08103-1701
1-800-257-8443 • 1-800-410-SOUP • 1-800-433-PACE
www.campbellsoup.com

137

Lazlo Toth
CALIFORNIA

1 1o 02

General Richard Myers
Chairman, Joint Chief of Staffs
The Pentagon
Washington, D.C.

Lazlo Toth
P.O. Box 245
Fairfax, California
94930 U.S.A.

Dear General Myers,

My new dentist went to Dental School in Kabul, and still has relatives living in Afganistan, and they wrote him that one thing that has changed since the war started, is that meat is much more plentiful.

But his Aunt is a little worried, and I told him I'd write to you to try to help him answer her question:

Is it safe to eat Goats, or other animals, that were killed in air strikes?   Does it make any difference if they were killed by a bomb or by a missile?

Lazlo Toth

1 April 2002

Mr. Lazlo Toth
Post Office Box 245
Fairfax, CA 94978

Dear Mr. Toth,

Thank you for the letter regarding conditions in Afghanistan. It is good to know that the situation has improved somewhat. Since the first of the year, food distribution has resumed and more people have been returning to their homes.

Please pardon the delay in answering. Your correspondence was just received due to safety precautions and new mail-handling procedures instituted following the anthrax threat in the Washington area.

Best wishes.

Sincerely,

RICHARD B. MYERS
Chairman
of the Joint Chiefs of Staff

Mr. Lazlo Toth
P.O. Box 245
Fairfax, CA 94978

December 24, 2001

Gloria E. Vivenzio
Director of Consumer Affairs
M&M's (Plain) Division of Mars, Inc.
Hakettstown, New Jersey 07840

Dear Director,

I'm sorry it's taken me so long to get back to you about your Millennium Promotion that ended on December 1, 1998.

All I know is I bought M&M's with the words, "INSTANTLY WIN $2,000,000" on the wrapper, <u>after</u> December 1, 1998.
Way way after!

How you can you sell a product that say's "Instantly <u>Win $2,000,000</u>" on the wrapper, knowing that it's <u>IMPOSSIBLE</u>!, because the contest was over, and there was already a "confirmed winner"?

Hopefully, we can clear all this is up if you'll just send me the name and address of the confirmed winner, and he'll be willing to split the money.

And, I'd like to deterine if he found the winning piece printed inside on the wrapper all by himself, or if he obtained the free game piece by reading the printed instructions in the lower left hand corner of the front wrapper which directed him to the instructions on the back telling him where to write to obtain the winning $2 million game piece without purchasing the product.

Also, I got out my magnifying glass and noticed the fine print inside the wrapper say's the $2 million is paid $100,000 per year over a period of 20 years, without interest.

How can you say "INSTANTLY WIN $2,000,000" if it takes 20 years to get it? My dictionary is in the ENGLISH language, and "<u>INSTANTLY</u>" means, "in an instant; without delay; immediately". It <u>doesn't mean</u>, "in the distance; delay; fudge.".

I have the feeling there are more lawyers working at M&M's now than there are people who make the chocolate, am I right? That's why I'm not going to drag this case out, and I'll do all I can to end this prior to the actual start of the proceedings.

Lazlo Toth

Congressman Dana Rohabacher
Foreign Relations Committee
U.S. House of Represenatives
Washington, D.C.

Dear Congressman Rohabacher,

A year ago you said on C Span that you thought Osama Bin Laden was "<u>Dead</u> and in Hell, and <u>not in heaven</u> with 70 dark eyed virgins".

I've often heard that Martyrs believe 70 virgins await them in Paradise, and I wonder if the meaning of the word "virgin" is as vague in the Arabic language as it is in English. If all it say's is "70 dark eyed virgins", he could end up with 70 dark eyed eighty year old nuns.

If it was me, I would want to see recent photographs of the waiting women and make it understood that they can't bring any of their relatives to live with us,- it's crowded enough just with the 71 of us!

All I need is 70 dark eyed Mother-in-laws moving in. Nobody needs 140 women always saying, "<u>somebody</u> forgot to put DOWN the toilet seat again".

<u>Question:</u>
I know when Moslems pray, they always pray facing towards Mecca. I wonder, in your studies of eschatology, if you ever learned what direction a Moslem faces when he is praying <u>in</u> Mecca. Also, do you know if there are tunnels underneath Mecca where someone and his wifes could hide?

Thank you for your knowledge, that's why we need you,

Laslo Toth

buffet
messina

Lazlo Toth
PO Box 245
Fairfax CA 94978-0245

2 . 18 . 02

President George W. Bush
The White House
Washington, D.C.

Dear President Bush,

        I saw your interview with Tom Brokaw, and what I found
most interesting were your comments about the ENRON swindle,
and about your relationship with the former CEO, Kenneth Lay.

        They say in the past you used to call him "Kenny Boy",
but you refer to him now as "Mister Lay", as though he was
somebody you may have met a few times, but wouldn't be able
to pick out of a lineup, especially if he was wearing a
cowboy hat.

        When Tom Brokaw said, "I understand even your Mother-
in-law lost money", you said, "Yes, but not much — eight
thousand dollars".

        $8,ooo? Not much?
        For your sake, I hope your Mother-in-law wasn't watching.

        Mr. President, I think you need a lesson in current
reality.
You've been hanging out with people like Dick Cheney for too
long. My advise to you —
        DON'T TRUST ANYONE who makes OVER THIRTY million dollars
a year. With one exception — Sandra Bullock.

        You should sit down and talk to Alan Greenspan, - ask
him how long it takes a middle tax bracket American family
to save $8,000.
        And don't expect him to agree with you that loosing
$8,000 is "not much". The man makes his own suits!   When
he's not in meetings at the Federal Reserve, he's home
sewing.

        And when your Mother-in-law starts talking to you
again, ask her if she thinks Mr. Kenny Boy should do time in
jail.
        I think she's going to say, "Yes, but not much — eight
years".

                              Lazlo Toth

'a scola sta finennu

1 20 20 02

Don Rumsfelt - Secretary of Defense
The Pentagon
Washington, D.C.

LAZLO TOTH
P.O. BOX 245
FAIRFAX, CA. 94978-0245

Dear Don Rumsfelt,

I had a dream I saw Osama Bin Laden, sitting on a mattress, underneath a big rock. And I said, "That doesn't look very safe, Osama", and he said, "Safe?, are you kidding me?, the <u>Barzini Family</u> has guranteed my safety".

And then I read that within the Qaaba, which is at the center of the Grand Mosque complex in Mecca, there is a meteorite, which people worshiped before the time of Mohammed, way before Islam even began.

I don't think you have to be born in Vienna to interpet the dream as meaning that he's gone to the mattresses, and the "rock" represents the grand mosque at Mecca, where he feels "safe" because he's under the protection of "the Barzini's" — the Saudi Royal Family! Personally, I think it was the Barzini's (House of al-Saud) behind the whole thing all along.

I don't know how much stock you put into dreams, but if I were you, I'd send a squad of special forces into Mecca to check it out — what can you loose?

I watched another one of your war briefings today and all I've got to say is <u>YOU</u> <u>ARE</u> <u>SMOOTH</u>.

<u>Here's some ideas for you to use at future briefings</u>:

<u>YOU</u>:- Yes, we've dropped over a hundred 15,000 ton bombs on about a hundred caves, and - okay, maybe we didn't get Osama, but I'll tell you this — we sure killed a lot of bats!

<u>YOU</u> - Has Osama and other top Talibans managed to sneak over the border to Pakistan? It's possible,
There Must Be<u> 50 Ways to Leave Afganistan</u>:
Hop on a mule, Abdul.
Dress as a maiden, Bin Laden.
Have your wives pull you in a sled, Akmed.
Give the border guards Moola, Mullah.
I'm got to leave now, I've got an important meeting with Prince Bandar. But General Myers here is going to read you the other 46 ways.

Don, If there's any man who can CONVINCE the American people that you're right, it's YOU. I swear, when you talk, it's like I hear feet tapping. It's like your tongue has cleats.

Bombs away!

ToTh AiR
We'LL Get You There

Fairfax Field   Suite 2-4-5   V   Fairfax. California   9 4978

Lazlo ToTh
PRESIDENT

01/02/2002   22:48

Hon. Albert Gore
Metropolitan West Financial Inc.
11440 San Vincente Blvd.
West Los Angeles, California

Dear AL,
    Congradulations on your new job. You made a smart move
getting out of teaching.
    Education is an esteemed profession, but Finance is the
cornerstone upon which money is made, and with all the
important people you know, I know you'll do great at
Metropolitan West Financial Inc., you must be excited.

    Once, years ago, I tried my hand at Global Money
Management, - in Geneva, with Investors Overseas Services.
    And even back then, Bernie Cornfelt hired one of FDR's
son's to work for I.O.S., so it's nothing new. Bernie would
have "The Roosevelt" call all his rich friends and say,
"Let's have lunch", then Bernie would always just show up and
join them, and when Roosevelt got up and went to the
bathroom, Bernie would do his pitch and sell Roosevelt's
friend a mutual fund. Then Bernie would wave and have
Roosevelt come back to the table.

    Anyway, let's catch up. I sold the film studio, but
stayed on as CEO, but those things never work out, the new
owner was a real dreamer, BUT!, getting out of there led me
to finally do what I've always wanted to do, and I write to
say, - I sit here tonight as my own airline!
    So far, it hasn't been easy, but, we're on our way!

    AL, I'm real proud of you, and I would like you to
manage my 401(K). I need to do a ROLLOVER, and if you would
share your knowledge, your experience will come in handy.
    My money is in a C.D.(Certificate of Deposit) at CAL FED,
at Calvary Shopping Center, at present, but, I don't like
their attitude. The manager tells me, "Even if there's a
depression we won't go under, and there will <u>never</u> be another
depression".
    Al, in an open ended universe, "never" is just a matter
of time. That's why, I'm transfering the funds over to you,
at maturity, regardless of the fee.

Tax deferred interest rules!,

Best!, Lazlo

Lazlo Toth

P.S. I hope you didn't forget to send Rosty Rostenkowski
    a birthday card. He's 74 or 75 years old today.

METWEST FINANCIAL

11440 San Vicente 3rd Floor   Los Angeles California 90049

tel 310 979 6300   fax 310 979 6399   web www.mwfin.com

February 5, 2003

Mr. Lazlo Toth
P.O. Box 245
Fairfax, CA 94978

Dear Mr. Toth:

We are in receipt of your letter asking about transferring your 401K Plan to us from Cal Fed. Unfortunately, you did not include a phone number and you are not listed so I could not call you.

MetWest Financial, LLC is a holding company of a family of financial services firms. Unfortunately, we do not handle individual accounts. However, MetWest Capital Management, an affiliate located in Newport Beach, California, specializes in equity and balanced portfolios for high net worth individuals. I am not certain of the size of your account, but it sounds as if you need to go to a retail brokerage firm.

We appreciate your interest and desire to invest with MetWest, but unfortunately, we cannot be of service to you.

Sincerely,

Janet S. Lee
Administrative Manager

Lazlo Toth

PO Box 245
Fairfax, California
94978

Mr. Ray Tater
Assistant Director
California Council for the Arts
Poet Laureat Department
State of California
1300 "I" Street
Sacramento, California 95814

Dear Mr. Tater,

     I would like to take this opportunity to noninate myself for the post of Califonia Poet Laureat.

     The poem I am submitting (<u>The Pumpkin in the Birdcage</u>) is one which I wrote for Senator John Glenn commemorating his return from outer space and subsequent participation in the Clinton Impeachment trial.

     He never wrote me back, so I am using the same poem for this purpose, but I have many other poems ready to go if you need them.

Lazlo Toth

Lazlo Toth

The PUMPKIN in the BIRDCAGE
(Poem for an Impeachment trial)

JOHN GLENN BACK
From   Outer Spa c e
EARTH
In His Face
F r a g i l e B e a u t y
UP TOOCLOSE

A S T R O senator J U R O R
M I S T
in the fog
T R U T H
never called
g r a v i t y
" H O M E S "

California
CALIFORNIA ARTS COUNCIL
Arts Council

CELEBRATING EXCELLENCE IN THE ARTS SINCE 1976

GRAY DAVIS, GOVERNOR

BARRY HESSENIUS, DIRECTOR

May 30, 2002

Lazlo Toth
P.O. Box 245
Fairfax, CA 94978

Dear Lazlo,

The California Arts Council is deeply honored to have received so many fine nominations for the post of Poet Laureate. We were challenged to review the best literary talents of our state. While the task of recommending only three names to the Office of the Governor was extremely difficult for the panelists, but they have chosen them for this round. Through independent panel reviews, the three names submitted this year are (in no special order): Francisco Alarcón, Diane Di Prima and Quincy Troupe.

It was a close vote. While your nomination is not among these, we trust that you know that your work is vital to the art form. The fact of your nomination demonstrates the high value placed by many on your poetry. Your efforts to make poetry a living part of our culture are appreciated. We hope you will let us keep your work on file, put the poems on our website with your picture and keep you abreast of the program as it develops. We see this as an ongoing effort. The program is designed so that the Laureate is chosen every 2 years. The Arts Council believes that 2 years will give each poet laureate time to envision and create a service to the art form that satisfies.

We hope you will join us in some way to support the poet laureate as an educator and advocate for writers, a symbol for civic and state leaders, a master teacher whose work embodies values and varieties of poetry that make up the great wealth of creative expression throughout our state. We will work to develop support for the program from all of California's poets.

Sincerely,

Ray Tatar

Ray Tatar
Literature Administrator
(916) 322-6395
rtatar@caartscouncil.com

California poet laureate Quincy Troupe had a stanza on his resume stating he graduated from Grambling College. He didn't. The Senate Rules Committee, preparing to confirm him, found the embellishment. Troupe resigned.

cc Barry Hessenius, Director

1300 I STREET, SUITE 930 · SACRAMENTO, CA 95814 · (916) 322-6555 · (800) 201-6201 · FAX (916) 322-6575 · WWW.CAC.CA.GOV

Knights of Serra

Mr. Lazlo Toth
P.O. Box 245
Fairfax, CA 94978-0245

His Excellancy
Cardinal Bernard Law
ArchBishop of Boston

July 12, 2002

Your Excellency,

      Two words - <u>Don't</u> <u>Resign</u>!
      You don't deserve this treatment!

      You remind me of the parable about the fish peddler who was
accused of selling (reassigning) fish he knew had gone bad. And even
after he got rid of all the bad fish, and promised he wouldn't do it
again, STILL!, nobody would buy fish from him. Why?   Because they
said he still SMELLED like bad fish. It's like you can't win
sometimes.

      Especially! if you have the protestant press hounding on your
heels! Oh, how they love bashing the Catholics! How about that hill
billy protestant crooner Jerry Lee Lewis? I guess it's okay to be a
pedophile as long as the fourteen-year-old is your Protestant <u>cousin</u>!
And how about the Mormons? They're all pedophiles! Do you know what
they call a 25-year-old woman at a Mormon wedding? The Mother of the
Bride!

      But!, all your problems will pass <u>LIKE A SCANDLE IN THE WIND</u>,
as Elton Johns may sing.
      Already, the headlines have shifted to the story about the
Forest Ranger who started his own fire, and the cameras that were
pouncing on you, are lurking in Martha Stewart's driveway now.
      Your Emmence, things are looking up, it's a whole new news day!

      The thing to post in your mind is the tradition of the position
you were blessed and burdened to uphold - the honor of wearing the
crown of ArchBishop of Boston. The mighty miter once worn by the great
Francis Cardinal Spellman, a grocers' son, who ended up controlling an
American Catholic Church worth $10 Billion.

      But, like you, he too had his critics. But, in the end, he
always won. They tell a story at the Gregorian that when he was a
young Priest some parishioners wrote to <u>his</u> Bishop accusing him of,
"always looking at his reflection in the chalice when he's saying
mass".   But he told the Bishop it might look to the people that he was
looking at himself, but actually, he was using the chalice as a mirror,
to look behind him to see if the ushers had begun to pass the
collection baskets.

      So, instead of being reprimanded for his narcissism, he was
promoted for his faithfulness (to financial matters), and was soon
picked to study in Rome. That's the road that led him to becoming best
friends with the hoy poloy of his time, including, His Holiness Pope
Pius XII, President Frankilin Roosevelt, and Merv Griffin.

                       I know we're both feeling better,

                         Toth

enclosed:
$5 cash for you to use however you see fit.

CARDINAL'S RESIDENCE
2101 COMMONWEALTH AVENUE
BRIGHTON, MASSACHUSETTS 02135

August 13, 2002

Mr. Lazlo Toth
P.O. Box 245
Fairfax, CA 94978

Dear Mr. Toth:

I deeply appreciate your letter of prayerful support.

These are particularly challenging days, and letters such as yours
provide great encouragement.

The task before us is clear. There is much to learn both from the
successes and the mistakes of the past. At the end of the day, the
Church will be helped in her ministry by the changes which are being
made here and throughout the country.

Thank you for the donation of $5.00 that was enclosed with your letter.
I want you to know that I have placed that money into the fund to
assist me in responding to the needs of the victims of sexual abuse by
clergy.

With warm personal regards and asking God to bless you, I am

Sincerely yours in Christ,

Archbishop of Boston

BCL/jrs

Mr. Lazlo Toth
P.O. Box 245
Fairfax, CA 94978-0245

September 30, 2002

Sir Alan Greenspan
Chairman Federal Reserve Board
Knight of the Royal Crown
Washington, D.C.

Dear Sir Alan,

My congradulations on being crowned a Knight by Queen
Elizabeth Windsor of England.

We thank God for all you have done to help the American
economy over the last few decades, but it's nice to see a
foreigner plant some recognition on your dusty boots as well.

But, I wouldn't be fair to myself if I didn't tell you
I think it's somewhat questionable WHY the Queen would make
Elton John a Knight <u>two years</u> before YOU.

And I heard she deceided against making <u>Herman and the
Hermits</u> Knights because they refused to fight in the the
Falklands. Maybe you were chosen to replace Herman.

I'd like to collaborate with Elton John on a special
song just for the Queen, to be called <u>Nostrils In the Wind</u>.

Regardless, Congradulations. I hear Barry Manilow is
going to be made one too, but not till next year, he was too
busy — working in Reno.

<u>Sir Alan, I need your help</u>. A few weeks ago I read that
you said you were "<u>GUARDEDLY OPTIMISTIC</u>" about the future of
the U.S. stock market. And about one year ago, you said you
were "<u>CAUTIOUSLY OPTIMISTIC</u>", at that time.

Sir Alan, between "<u>Guardedly</u> Optimistic" and
"<u>CAUTIOUSLY</u> OPTIMISTIC", which one is <u>more</u> optimistic than
the other one?

Which is worse, now or then?

I can't tell if it's your goal to make people feel
Guardedly confused, or just Cautiously confused.

Vertically functioning,

Lazlo Toth

Lazlo Toth

TOTH COCKTAIL SAUCE COMPANY
Makers of "ANCHORS AHOY!" Tar Tar Sauce

LAZLO TOTH
C.E.O.

Mr. Lazlo Toth
P.O. Box 245
Fairfax, CA 94978-0245

November 2, 2002

U.S. Navy Rear Admiral Ret. MARSHA JOHNSON
National Executive Director <u>GIRL SCOUTS of the USA</u>
C/o Parade Magazine - 711 3rdAve. N.Y.,N.Y.

Dear Admiral,
    I saw your picture on the cover of <u>Parade Magazine</u>.
Every Sunday, I read it cover to cover. Congradulations!

    I've only been in the cocktail sauce bussiness
(professionally) for less than a year, but I have an
inventory opportunity for your organization (GIRL SCOUTS)
and I'm hoping we may find common ground in a partnership.

    I've been in conversations recently with Laurence Barnes,
a highly regarded mollusk merchant from Tomalas Bay, who does
shellfish harvesting on a seasonal (private contractor) basis
for the <u>Sir Francis Drake Oyster Company</u>, (I'm sure you've
heard of SIr Francis Drake, since you were in the Navy).
    Mr. Barnes and I would like to offer your organization a
businesss plan from which we all can prosper.

    Since your organization is already geared up to sell
cookies once a year, <u>GIRL SCOUT OYSTERS</u>, would be a seaworthy
addition for your door to door sales force, as well as a
natural extension for you personally, because of your Navy
background.
    And here's the big advantage for the GIRL SCOUTS — the
girls will <u>only take the orders</u>, there's no need for them to
go back to DELIVER the oysters in person. After they turn in
the orders to their Scout Master, the Oysters will be sent
via FIRST CLASS Mail, ICE PRIOIRTY, and all profits split
evenly between <u>GIRL SCOUTS OF USA</u>, <u>TOTH COCKTAIL SAUCE CO.</u>,
and <u>LARRY'S SHELLFISH COMMUNE</u>.

    I think it's smart to start with a limited number of
Scouts (Approx: 200), in a medium size fresh water market -
like Toledo, Ohio, or Buffalo, N.Y.
    After our initial TEST CITY, we'll be able to FINE TUNE
things before we branch out nationally.

    To help the girls, as a sales aide, my suggestion is
that the GIRL SCOUTS purchase COCKTAIL SAUCE, which they can
give FREE to customers when they order a dozen (or more)
Oysters.
    At this time, I have 1,062 bottles of top quality Tar
Tar Sauce that still has almost six months to go before the
expiration date comes due.
    I'm willing to make as many as 1,050 jars of my TAR TAR
inventory available, at a very good discount, in order to
expedite the launch of our new venture. COME ABOARD!,

Lazlo Toth

TOTH UPHOLSTERY COMPANY
Specializing in Seat Covers for Miniature Cars
" No car is too small for seat covers."
_____
Lazlo Toth
President

November 12, 2002

Rep. Kathern Harris
Republican — Florida
UNITED STATES House of Representatives
Washington, D.C.

Dear Congressperson HARRIS,

SHEEPSKIN,
LAMBSKIN,
zebra
and
LEOPARD
PATTERNS
AVAILABLE
FOR
miniature
CARS
FROM
TWELVE
TO
ONE
INCH
LONG.

Congrats on your election to the U.S. Congress!
And thanks for all your help in the past in helping to put George W. Bush in the White House, where he belongs! — please, Stand Up! Thank you.
Your election to congress was like icing on the cake for President Bush's well deserved mid term triumph! - stand up again! And this time, don't sit down.
Why? Because I read that his brother, Zep, won too. What a coup!
And also, Elizabeth Dole!
What a day! Thank you. Sit.

I heard that the only reason Elizabeth Dole ran for the Senate in the first place was to get away from her Viagra "incessant" husband.
"Bob!, do I have to get a restraining order from the DCPD, or run for the Senate from North Carolina, to get you to LEAVE ME ALONE?!".
That's what they say she kept warning him, but HE JUST DIDN'T GET IT!
Neighbors in the Watergate apartments say her voice carried. "NO!, I don't want TEA!,..GO AWAY!".
And <u>his</u> voice carried, too.
"Elizabeth!, can't we just talk this over like adults?", he would shout.
"Let me in, come on, the tea's getting cold,..I just want to.. just TALK, I promise,.. Elizabeth!, it's Chamomile.".
And now, I heard somebody is already writing a book about her campaign. It's called: <u>M O R N I N G W O O D.</u>
<u>The Story Behind One Woman's Desire</u>
<u>to Run for the United States Senate.</u>

Kid
Leather
MINIATURE
STEERING
WHEEL
COVERS

_____ <u>But, On to BUSINESS!:</u>
I'm thinking of sending some of my clients FLORIDA ORANGES as Holiday GIFTS, and I wonder if you could recommend a responsible orange company to handle the job. <u>One Thing! It's</u> <u>important to me that the ORANGES are properly fumigated.</u>
Also, if it cost extra for FUMIGATION, that's a factor, but, WORKING TOGETHER, with LUCK, we can make this work.

DON'T
JUST
SIT
THERE
UP
GRADE
your
collection
NOW!

Keep doing a great job,

Lazlo Toth

Mr. Lazlo Toth
P.O. Box 245
Fairfax, CA 94978

LAZLO TOTH

CALIFORNIA

Lazlo Toth
P.O. Box 245
Fairfax
California 94978

2

Postmaster Geneal
U.S. Postal Service
475 L'Enfant Plaza SW
Wahington.d.c. 20260-

<u>RE: INCLOSED LETTER</u>

Dear General,

Something has come up that I think you should be
briefed about.

I wrote a letter recently to Alan Greenspan, the
Chairman of the Federal Reserve Board, and it was returned
to me marked "ATTEMPTED UNKNOWN".

That's the biggest crock I've ever heard.

He's the <u>Chairman</u> of the Fedreal Reserve, I can't
believe you did this to him.

Something is WRONG when an American like Greenspans
is honored and made into a Royal Knight in one coutry,
and then treated like a used postage stamp in his own.

Mr. Postmaster, General!, the stock market is on
shacky ground as it is, he's trying his best to manage
things, PLEASE let's not let this grow into a sceeaming
match between Greenspan and the postal workers. It's just
not worth it.

Thanks for helping me get to the bottom of this.

Lazlo Toth III

Please keep me posted,

JOTH
PO BOX 245
FairfAX Calf.
94978

MOVED LEFT NO ADDRESS
FORWARDING ORDER EXPIRED
NO SUCH STREET NUMBER
UNDELIVERABLE AS ADDRESSED
ATTEMPTED UNKNOWN

ATLANTA GA
PM
19 OCT
2002

3635   D56

Sir Alan Greenspan
Federal Reserve Chairman
2001 "C" Street
Washington. D/C.

2/6710

UNITED STATES POSTAL SERVICE

n being
watched

an
WRITER

ill be cast-
shington,
this week
leral gov-
do to re-
y.
the Fed-
hat sets
oday for
's stock
lease of

DOUG MILLS / Associated Press

Fed chairman Alan Greenspan
and colleagues will meet today.

December 26, 2002

Mr. Lazlo Toth
Post Office Box 245
Fairfax, CA 94978-0245

Dear Mr. Toth:

Thank you for writing Postmaster General John E. Potter, who has referred your letter to this office. I understand your concern and appreciate the opportunity to answer your questions. The main function of the Postal Service and its core business is delivery of the mail and every reasonable effort is made every day to do just that.

Mail frequently enters the postal system with an incomplete or incorrect address. At other times, mail is addressed to a physical location that is not an approved delivery point. Although processes exist to improve address quality, all postal employees must remember that if the customer and delivery point are known, the Postal Service's fundamental organizational purpose is to deliver that mail--regardless of class and when the customer's correct address is known--unless the mail piece specifies other delivery instructions. The objective is not to return or dispose of mail unless it is absolutely necessary. The "local knowledge" of our carriers and clerks often helps with a successful delivery.

Of course, the sure way of getting our best possible service is for you to use complete, accurate, and legible addresses. As more and more mail is sorted by automation, the absence of a complete address is sure to hinder delivery of your important mail. Also, mail is often processed in a facility that is distant from the town to which your mail may be addressed. When there is uncertainty about the correct address, we believe it is better to return the mail to its sender, rather than risk delivery to the wrong person.

Addressing Tips:
Write, type, or print the complete address neatly.
ALWAYS use a complete return address.
Always use complete address information; such as Ave., Blvd., and St
Always use the apartment or suite number. Alw___
such as N. W. and SW

We know how important your mail is to you, Mr. Toth. Taking a few minutes to prepare it carefully and correctly makes a lot of sense and will enable us to give you and the addressee much better service. I am sorry for the disappointment and inconvenience the return caused.

Sincerely,

Vanessa Williams

Vanessa Williams
Consumer Support Specialist

Reference:W45034947

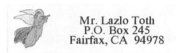

Mr. Lazlo Toth
P.O. Box 245
Fairfax, CA 94978

Royal Queen Highness   Elizabeth (Windsor)
Queen of English Empire
Buckingham Palace
London, England

Dear your Royal Highness,

    Merry Christmas and a Happy New Year 2003 from all your
loyal royal fans in America, Stand Up!, Hip! Hip! Horray!

    I had a dream that I must pass on to you. How you will
deal with it is up to you, I am just the messenger conduit.

    I dreamed a crowd of people were chanting, "Charles!,
Charles, we need you!- now! Charles!, we need you now!".

    In my Dream <u>the whole world was waiting</u> for your Son,
royal Crown Prince Charles, to mount the thrown so the world
could be healed.

    "They will call him <u>The Calm King</u>", a woman in white told
me, and everyone standing behind her smiled.

    Highness!, I have made you a painting of the future King
to commemorate the message.

    You know I adore you, but I think you should follow the
wishes of the masses and make your son Charles the King of
England <u>now</u>.

    We need him, and everyone knows he's as ready as he's
ever going to be.

                            ~~your cousin,~~

                            Lazlo Toth

                            Lazlo Toth

    P.S.
    I wanted to get my painting framed for you, but the postage
would be prohibitive, so I have inclosed some money for you
to get it done over there.
    inclosed: $4.

TOTH

LAZLO TOTH
P.O. BOX 245
FAIRFAX, CA. 94978-0245

Corrado Cardinal Bafile
Prefect, Congregation for the Causes of Saints
Vatican City, (state)

I - II - M M III

Venerable Eminence,

I got your name from my pastor before he was reassigned.

I write this letter on behalf of a woman who is currectly legally named <u>Constanza L. Winslow</u>.

On a recent visit to Mexico, she was bitten by the most deadly fish known to man - The venamous "Poison Lurk Monk Fish", or "The Lurking Monk of Mazatlan". Like a chameleon, it has the ability to change colors, and its biggest trick is turning BLUE, and disguising itself as <u>water</u>.

If you get bit by one, your chances of survival are one hundred million to one (the same as the chances of getting hit by LIGHTENING <u>and</u> attacked by killer bees on the same day). So far, no one has ever survived the bite of a Mazatlan Lurking Monkfish - until Ms. Winslow (Lupe).

After she was attacked, all she could remember was praying to <u>Mother Teresa of Calcutta,</u> and dogpaddling as fast as she could. And next thing she remembers, she's standing in line at some Mexican HMO, almost in a coma.

She says if it wasn't for <u>Mother Teresa of Calcutta</u> she never would have made it.

I understand that a Nun in India had a cystic tumor cured by Mother Teresa, and that if she gets <u>one more</u> miracle, the Pope is going to break the rules and make her a Saint <u>immediately</u>.

So, I think this could be IT!. Someone should tell him.

I know you'll want all the medical records, and that will be no problem, Mexico is known for keeping good records. I just hope they'll be reasonably priced.

And should we have them translated into Latin, or can we just send you copies of the originals?

Also, we have the name of the life guard who witnessed the whole thing, and I am making arrangements for a phone call to link him up with a Spanish speaking notary public, who will obtain his sworn testimony on a tape recorder, which we will hook up to the phone.

<u>   One problem: our only glitch</u>. Right after I heard Lupe was bit by the Mazatlan Lurking Monkfish, I had a friend look it up on the WEB, and when he told me her chances of survival were ZILCH, I said a prayer to <u>Fr. Junipero Serra</u> of San Jose, asking him to help her.

Now, how do we know for sure it wasn't Father Serra that did the miracle and not Mother Teresa? My prayer wasn't very long, and I wasn't splashing around BEGGING like Lupe was, but how do we know for sure which did the miracle?

We were hoping BOTH Mother Teresa AND Fr. Serra could get credit for one each, and both could be made Saints <u>NOW</u>.

We can come to Rome whenever you need us. Toth

Toth
Freelance

Advertising
Advice
All purpose

December 10, 2002

President Cantalupo
President McDonald's Corporation
Oak Brok, Illinois

Lazlo Toth
P.O. Box 245
Fairfax, California
USA 94978

Dear President Cantalupo.

Congradulations on being named the 5th President of McDonald's.
I think Jack Greenberg (#4) did a good job when he was in there,
but he was no Ray Kroc – number one!
But I think where Greenberg made his big mistake was introducing
the McTaco. That was his downfall. Nobody wants to go to McDoanld's
for Mexican food. I wonder what he had to eat the night he dreamed
that one up. Besides it being a stupid idea, people said it tasted like a
hockey puck with salsa on it.

I've got a great idea for a new product for you to kick off your
administration. And although I've worked some with the Burger King
people, this idea is exclusive to McDonald's, it's the way I like to work.

__The Preamble:__
Lately the press and the health nuts have been coming down hard
on the food industry, blaming you guys for the reason a lot of people
in America are getting fatter.
__The Product:__
I have an idea to recapture the south of the border spirit you lost
with Greenberg's misguided McTaco, that, at the same time, one ups
the health food nuts. Yes!, - It's Lean! and - it's Latin!
I call my ground beef brainchild - ! The McNada!.
It's a Low Fat Hamburger on a Plain Bun with Nothing On It.

! Loose weight the McNada way !
Get your McCulo down to McDonald's.
! The McNada !
THERE'S Nada LIKE IT

Mr. Cantalupo, I'm hoping we can do a lot of business together
during your tenure, and as a welcoming gift to you, I'm willing to give
you full rights to this product idea for $500 IF you can FED EX me the
money by next Friday.

Laylo Toth

McDonald's Corporation
McDonald's Plaza
Oak Brook, Illinois 60523-1900
Direct Dial Number

(800) 244-6227

January 02, 2003

Mr. Lazlo Toth
PO Box 245
Fairfax, CA   94978-0245

Dear Mr. Toth:

Thank you for contacting McDonald's recently with your idea for a product or service that you believe would be of interest to us. We appreciate your interest in McDonald's, but we have to return the material you sent us because it is our company's policy not to consider unsolicited ideas from outside the McDonald's system.

It's not that great ideas cannot come from people outside of McDonald's. Each year, however, McDonald's receives thousands of unsolicited ideas and proposals for products and services from individuals as well as companies. Because of the volume of unsolicited ideas and the difficulty of sorting out what is truly a "new" idea as opposed to a concept that has already been considered or developed by McDonald's, we must adhere to a strict policy of not reviewing any unsolicited ideas that come from outside the McDonald's family of employees, franchisees and approved suppliers. We realize that we may be missing out on a few good ideas, but we have had to adopt this policy for legal and business reasons.

As a result, we must decline your invitation to review your submission and hope you understand the reasons for this decision. Enclosed is your original submission. Your material has not been reviewed, and we are retaining no copies.

Again, Mr. Toth, thank you for thinking of McDonald's.

Sincerely

Rob Beard
Consumer Response Representative
McDonald's Customer Satisfaction Department
ref#:1134171

McDonald's posts first loss ever

first time since 1995. $350 milli...

FREELANCETOTH

graphic needs met ●   In a **/** slash

LAZLO TOTH

January 6, 2003

Mr. Rob Beard
Mcdonald's Corporation
Dept. of Consumer Response & Satisfaction
Ronald McDonald Plaza
Oak Brook, Illinois 6 0 5 2 3

Lazlo Toth
P.O. Box 245
Fairfax, California
USA 94978

Dear Mr. Beard,

      #1. Your company is going down the tubes of history, you should take ideas from anyone who will give them to you.

      #2. You had no right opening my letter to Canatlupo. It was private, and I think that's against the law on a federal level, if I'm not mistaken.

But!, regardless, I can take a hint. You're telling me that McDonald's has no interest in introducing a low calorie, south of the border burger like my McNada. I hear you.

Maybe this new sandnwich design is more up your Archway:

THE ONE HALF POUND
McDonald's McPORKER
TWO 1/4 lbs. WIENERS on a DOUBLE WIDE BUN
Pork that pulls no Punches

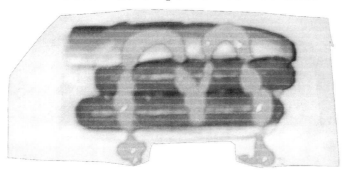

Ground Beef is a Meat for Losers.
ARCH Up!   The McPorker   ARCH Up!
THE HUMMER of SANDWICHES

Toth

Lazlo Toth
P.O. Box 245
Fairfax, CA 94978-0245

IMPORTANT

January 10, 2003

TOP SECRET

President
Campbell Soup Company
Camden, New Jersey   08103

Dear Mr. President,

    I have an idea that will make your ALPHABET SOUP,
<u>more</u> than <u>20% more profitable</u>.

    <u>How?</u> By downsizing the alphabet.

    Instead of having 26 different Noodles of the alphabet,
I cut the recipe down to 10.

        T<u>wo</u> A's :   **A**   **A**

    and <u>one each</u> of: **N**   **D**   **Y**

                W   **R**   **H**   **O** and **L**.

    It is my belief that this <u>NEW! ALPHABET SOUP</u>
will appeal to those people who like **<u>A N D Y   W A R H O L</u>**,
as well as to people who don't like the <u>ALPHABET</u>.
And I'm one of both.

    <u>Andy Warhol</u> is to soup what Picasso is to cubes.
Face it, the best thing about your soup was his painting.

    And, a lot of people hate the <u>ALPHABET</u>. It's too linear.
The worst is when people start <u>singing</u> it,- it's <u>meaningless</u>.
It's like listening to <u>One Hundred Bottles Of Beer on the
Wall</u> without the lyrics.

    Please give <u>Andy Warhol Aphabet Soup</u> its fifteen minutes
in the sun, you owe it to him.

Lazlo Toth

Have your own 15 minutes of soup.

Campbell Soup Company

January 17, 2003

Mr. Lazlo Toth
PO Box 245
Fairfax, CA 94978

Dear Mr. Toth:

Thank you for taking the time to contact us with your suggestion. We very much appreciate your enthusiasm for our Company and our products.

In an effort to continually build our business at Campbell Soup Company, our marketing, advertising, and research staff work with our various advertising agencies and consultants to constantly evaluate our products, packaging, advertising and marketing strategies.

As a result and in order to avoid misunderstandings with members of the public who wish to submit ideas for possible new technology, products, packaging, advertising or marketing concepts, we regretfully do not review these ideas on an ad hoc basis. I am sure you will understand that in order to avoid any potential conflict of interest we must return all communication with you.

Thank you for your interest in our Company and we wish you the best of luck in the future.

Sincerely,

Alcides Nieto
Consumer Services Representative

1718383A

CONSUMER RESPONSE AND INFORMATION CENTER • CAMDEN, NEW JERSEY 08103-1701
1-800-257-8443 • 1-800-410-SOUP • 1-800-433-PACE
WWW.CAMPBELLSOUP.COM

164

ToTh AiR

We'll Get There

P.O.B. 245 . Fairfax V California . 94978

Lazlo Toth
PRESIDENT

06/07/2003

FISHER NUT DIVISION
JOHN B. SANFILLIPPO AND SONS, INC.
ELK GROVE VILLAGE, ILL. 60007

Dear Mr. Sanfilippo,

I once heard Richard Brandson of Virgin Airlines say
that he knew of a sure way for someone to become a
Millionare. He said, "Be a Billionaire and start an
airline".

I haven't lost millions (yet), but, believe me, starting
up an airline is not easy. To say that I'm behind schedule
is putting it mildly. According to my business plan, I
should be ordering the peanuts by now, but instead, I'm still
chumming for financing.

But, to make a long story short, I've deceided to go
ahead and order the peanuts. I figure that besides getting
our name out there, if people like the peanuts, we're
building up a good reputation for when we get in the air.

Brandson hasn't got back to me yet with information on
what nut company he uses, but I know your company packages
peanuts for AMERICAN AIRLINES as well as SOUTHWEST, and yours
are the kind of top quality nuts I seek.

Mr. Sanfillippo, when management makes the decision to
put the peanuts before the planes, one thing is certain — the
nuts better be good. That's why I hope your fine company can
work with me to get things rolling.

This is the basic ART WORK my design team has come up
with, and we would like the package the same color BLUE you
did for American Airlines.

What's the minimum order that could financially make
sense for both of us? I have already talked to two stores
who promised me they would sell them, BUT! they made me
promise the nuts would have an expiration date on the
package, so that's a necessity.

Also, I'm assuming all price quotes will include SALT,

Lazlo Toth

T=H=E w=a=T=T T=H=A=T M=A=T=T=E=R=S

CONFIDENTIAL   Radio 1 waTT

=====   __   POB 245 94978 USA   **Lazlo Toth**
         ==   =   = World Desk =

Saddam Hussein
c/o Baath Party Headquarters
Bagdad, Iraq   <u>16 JU NE 03</u>

Dear Saddam, Hussein!,

    I write this letter knowing that you may never read it,
but I'm investing my hopes in the thought that some former
Baath party postal mole may have weaseled his way back into
the postal service and he'll be able to pass this letter on
to someone who knows someone who knows where you're currently
mattressing down (laying low).
    I know it's a long shot, but this is important.

    Hussein, I hate to be the one to have to break it to
you, but there has been <u>more</u> than a lot of bad press here
recently concerning your son, UDAY, - the tall one.

    If he had some other Father, they would call him a "bad
seed", BUT! in his case, I think the saying, "the apple does
not fall far from the apple tree" is more <u>aparently</u> apropos.

    But, be calm, Saddam, because - <u>He may not be ALL YOUR
FAULT.</u> There may be a <u>clinical reason</u> for his dramatic
behavior — it's called BIPOLAR DISORDER, and, it's a great
excuse.

    My guess is that you probably have a few imbedded
licensed physicians with you there, in your bunker, and my
advise is that you get Uday, as well as yourself, checked
out as soon as possible.

    With all your money, you'll be able to hire the best
American lawyers, and instead of having to go before an
International Tribunal, they'll be able to have trial
transferred to a place where your behavior has been less in
the news — my suggestion, Modesto, California.

    And I'll bet you're pond of attorney's (The Impossible
Dream Team) will be able to get you off with just having to
do thirty days at the Betty Ford Clinic.

                                    Lazlo Toth

                                    Lazlo Toth

About the Author

Besides being Lazlo Toth, Don Novello is
also known as Father Guido Sarducci.